D1686041

Less T

The Case for a Falling Price
Level in a Growing Economy

George Selgin

Professor of Economics
Terry College of Business
University of Georgia

Published by The Institute of Economic Affairs
1997

First published in March 1997 by
The Institute of Economic Affairs
2 Lord North Street
Westminster
London SW1P 3LB

© THE INSTITUTE OF ECONOMIC AFFAIRS 1997

Hobart Paper 132
All rights reserved
ISSN 0073-2818
ISBN 0-255 36402-4

Printed in Great Britain by
Hartington Fine Arts Limited, Lancing, West Sussex
Set in Baskerville Roman 11 on 12 point

Contents

FOREWORD

One of main features of the 'counter-revolution' in economics which has resulted in the revival of classical liberal ideas has been a change in views about government's ability to control the economy. 'Fiscal fine tuning' is virtually discredited and monetary policy is no longer seen as a means of stimulating employment. Not just theory, but experience in many countries demonstrates that unemployment cannot for long be held below its 'natural' rate by monetary expansion. The proper rôle of monetary authorities is now generally regarded as keeping the general price level under control.

As economists' views have changed and attention has switched from employment-promotion to price stability, so inflation has been checked in many countries to the extent that zero inflation now appears an achievable goal. But is a stable price level the ideal? That is the fundamental question which Professor George Selgin asks in Hobart Paper 132.

Professor Selgin argues instead for a monetary policy which would allow prices to vary with movements in productivity (either labour or total factor productivity). Rather than attempting to keep the general price level constant, a 'productivity norm' policy would permit that level to change to reflect variations in unit costs of production. The consequence, as Selgin points out, would in recent times have been year-on-year price declines rather than the inflation which has been experienced. In the 30 years after the Second World War, for example, United States consumer prices would have halved instead of almost tripling.

Adverse supply shocks (such as harvest failures or wars) would be allowed to influence prices under a productivity norm. But the long-run tendency, in an economy with growing productivity, would be '...secular deflation interrupted by occasional negative supply shocks'(p. 70).

Selgin claims that the case for a productivity norm - which can be found in the writings of early 19th century writers - was all but lost in the Keynesian revolution and its aftermath. So, when monetarists again argued that price level control should be the prime aim of monetary policy,

5

'...they did so by rehabilitating old arguments for a constant price level, leaving the productivity norm alternative buried in obscurity'. (p. 13)

He goes on to develop the argument for the productivity norm, using both theory and historical evidence. In his view, the 'menu' (physical and managerial) costs of changing prices are likely to be less under such a norm than under a zero inflation régime; it is less likely to induce 'monetary misperception effects'; 'efficient outcomes using fixed money contracts' are more likely; and the real money stock will probably be closer to its optimum.

Some puzzling episodes in economic history are also addressed by Professor Selgin who argues, for example, that a falling price level '...is not necessarily a sign or source of depression' (p. 49). As he points out, the 'Great Depression' of 1873 to 1896 - when British wholesale prices fell by about a third - was actually a time of rising real incomes. Thus the Great Depression, '...considered as a depression of anything *except* the price level, appears to be a myth' (p. 51).

Under a productivity norm, the monetary authorities would target nominal income, setting its growth rate at the weighted average of labour (or labour and capital) input growth rates. Selgin contends that a productivity norm policy would be best implemented under a fully deregulated 'free' banking system which has an automatic tendency to stabilise nominal income.

It is an interesting commentary on the distance most countries have come in conquering inflation that the idea of the productivity norm has been revived. As Professor Selgin says:

'...zero inflationists have been busy wrestling with arguments for secular inflation. Not long ago they confronted a world economy hooked on double-digit inflation, where any proposal for reducing inflation was regarded as a recipe for depression, and where proposals for zero inflation were considered both cruel and utopian.'(p. 70)

That world has changed and it is now appropriate to question the zero inflation aim to determine whether or not it can be bettered.

The conclusions of this *Hobart Paper*, like those of all Institute publications, are those of the author and not of the Institute (which has no corporate view), its Trustees, Advisers or Directors. Professor Selgin's Paper is published as a thought-provoking and radical attempt to move forward the debate about the proper rôle of monetary policy and how the general level of prices should be controlled.

March 1997   COLIN ROBINSON
Editorial Director, The Institute of Economic Affairs;
Professor of Economics, University of Surrey

THE AUTHOR

George Selgin earned his PhD at New York University, and has taught at George Mason University and the University of Hong Kong. He is presently an Associate Professor of Economics at the University of Georgia.

Professor Selgin's published writings include *The Theory of Free Banking: Money Supply under Competitive Note Issue* (1988) and *Bank Deregulation and Monetary Order* (1996).

ACKNOWLEDGEMENTS

Several people have helped me to write this Paper, both by reviewing early drafts and by shaping my basic beliefs (often through polite but firm disagreement) concerning how the price level ought to behave. In particular I wish to thank Kevin Dowd, Milton Friedman, Kevin Hoover, David Laidler, William Lastrapes, Hugh Rockoff, Richard Timberlake, David Van Hoose, Lawrence H. White, and Leland Yeager, for their thoughtful suggestions and criticism.

G.S.

I. INTRODUCTION

'To a simple fellow like myself it seems that the lower prices which increased production makes possible would benefit everybody, but I recognise there must be a flaw in my thinking, for increased productivity has not brought – and does not seem likely to bring – lower prices. Presumably there is some good reason for this. Will someone explain?'[1]

Not long ago, many economists were convinced that monetary policy should aim at achieving 'full employment'. Those who looked upon monetary expansion as a way to eradicate almost all unemployment failed to appreciate that persistent unemployment is a non-monetary or 'natural' economic condition, which no amount of monetary medicine can cure. Today most of us know better: both theory and experience have taught us that trying to hold unemployment below its 'natural rate' through monetary expansion is like trying to relieve a hangover by having another drink: in both cases, the prescribed cure eventually makes the patient worse off.[2]

Heeding this 'natural rate' perspective, several governments – including those of Great Britain, the US, Canada, Australia, and New Zealand – have taken or are considering steps to relieve their central banks of responsibility for creating jobs, allowing them to focus instead on something central banks *can* do: limiting movements in the general level of output prices. This new trend in monetary policy raises a question of fundamental importance to both economists and policy makers: how should we want the price level to behave?

Many if not most economists today view a constant output price level or 'zero inflation' as both a theoretical and a

---

[1] A former Archbishop of Wales, in a letter to the London *Times*, as quoted in Robertson (1963, pp. 11-12n).

[2] Past attempts by central banks to 'cure' unemployment and stimulate economic growth through inflation have tended to heighten 'natural' unemployment rates and reduce growth by misdirecting labour and other resources (Hayek, 1975; Cozier and Selody, 1992).

practical ideal.[3] Even some of the more determined critics of a zero inflation policy seem prepared to admit its theoretical merits, opposing it solely on the grounds that *getting* to zero would be excessively costly.[4]

I believe that zero inflationists are wrong for reasons having nothing to do with transition costs. I am inclined to agree with zero inflationists' claim that the long-run benefits from any credible zero inflation policy, considered as a substitute for today's creeping inflation, would probably exceed that policy's short-run costs.[5] Nonetheless I submit that a constant price level, even once in place, would be far from ideal. Instead, the price level should be allowed to vary to reflect changes in goods' unit costs of production. I call a pattern of general price level adjustments corresponding to such a rule for individual price changes a 'productivity norm'. Under a productivity norm, changes in velocity would be prevented (as under zero inflation) from influencing the price level through offsetting adjustments in the supply of money. But adverse 'supply shocks' like wars and harvest failures would be allowed to manifest themselves in higher output prices, while permanent improvements in productivity would be allowed to lower prices permanently.

Economists employ two different notions of productivity – labour productivity and total factor productivity[6] – and

---

[3] Some authors distinguish between a constant price level and zero inflation. But a genuine 'zero inflation' policy achieves a long-run, constant value for the price level by requiring the monetary authorities to 'roll back' the price-level whenever it changes from some initial value. (The alternative of 'letting bygones be bygones' is consistent with zero *expected* inflation only.) Most advocates of 'zero inflation' do in fact have a 'roll back' policy in mind. Thus William T. Gavin (1990, pp. 43-4) defines 'zero inflation' as being 'equivalent to a [stable] price level target', rejecting the alternative of zero expected inflation because, under this alternative, 'the price level would have no anchor [and] would drift about in response to real shocks and control errors'.

[4] Thus Canadian economist Robert F. Lucas (1990, p. 66), in arguing for living with some (4 per cent) inflation, writes: 'If the inflation rate can be chosen independent of history, then zero is clearly the preference of most, if not all, mainstream economists.' (Lest there should be any confusion, Robert *E.* Lucas, the American Nobel laureate, supports a goal of zero inflation.)

[5] Howitt (1990) and Carlstrom and Gavin (1993) offer effective replies to the 'transition cost' argument against zero inflation.

[6] Labour productivity is the ratio of real output to labour input, whereas total factor productivity is the ratio of real output to total factor (in practice, labour

disagree about how each should be measured. But one fact at least is beyond dispute: throughout modern history, improvements in aggregate productivity have overshadowed occasional setbacks. This has been especially true during the last half-century. According to one widely-used estimate, from 1948 to 1976 total factor productivity in the US grew by an average annual rate of 2 per cent.[7] Had a (total factor) productivity norm been in effect during this time, US consumer prices in 1976 would on average have been roughly half as high as they were just after the Second World War.[8] Instead, as Figure 1 shows, the US price level nearly tripled, obscuring the reality of falling real unit production costs. Other industrialised nations, including the UK, experienced both higher rates of inflation and more rapid productivity growth than the US, so for them the discrepancy between the progress of economic efficiency and that of money prices was

---

and capital) input. Algebraically, the (logarithmic) growth rate of labour productivity is equal to the growth rate of total factor productivity plus the growth rate of the capital-labour ratio multiplied by capital's share of total expenditures. Because production in most nations has tended to become more capital-intensive over time, labour productivity has tended to grow more rapidly than total factor productivity. See the Appendix (below, pp. 72-3) for details.

7 Bureau of Labor Statistics (1983). Kendrick and Grossman place the growth rate at 2·3 per cent, while Dale Jorgenson places it at only 1·3 per cent. Although different sources arrive at substantially different estimates of *average* productivity growth, it is worth noting that productivity time series from all of them are highly correlated. Norsworthy (1984) favours Jorgenson's techniques on account of their greater consistency with neo-classical economic theory. Other researchers (e.g. Levitan and Werneke, 1984, pp. 14-23) point to a downward bias inherent in available data. The BLS estimates may, therefore, be about right after all. For a comparison of alternative measurements of total factor productivity see Bureau of Labor Statistics, 1983, pp. 73-80.

8 That is a conservative estimate, which fails to allow for any adverse effect of inflation or deflation on productivity. In fact, there is a strong, negative empirical relation between the growth rate of productivity and the rate of inflation (Sbordone and Kuttner, 1994). Although causation might run either way, there are good reasons for suspecting, as Arthur Okun did (1980, p. 353,n15), 'that curbing inflation would do more to revive productivity than a direct stimulus to productivity could do to slow inflation'. Studies suggesting that the suspicion is warranted include Jarrett and Selody (1982) and Smyth (1995). Jarrett and Selody claimed in 1982 that a permanent 1 per cent reduction in the annual inflation rate would have raised US productivity growth by 0·11 percentage points.

11

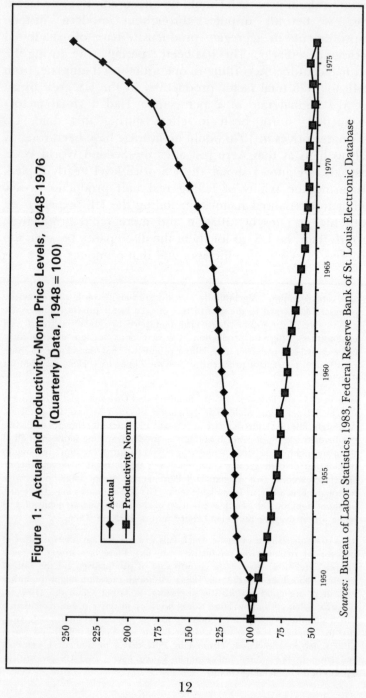

Figure 1: Actual and Productivity-Norm Price Levels, 1948-1976
(Quarterly Data, 1948 = 100)

Legend:
◆ Actual
■ Productivity Norm

Sources: Bureau of Labor Statistics, 1983, Federal Reserve Bank of St. Louis Electronic Database

even more severe. A policy of 'zero inflation' would partially have avoided this odd result. But only partially: even zero inflation would have involved some failure of money price signals to reflect transparently and accurately the true state and progress of real production possibilities.

Most of the arguments for a productivity norm are far from new. Many can be traced to economic writings of the early 19th century, and were a staple of both classical and neo-classical economic analysis. Prominent economists who made these arguments included David Davidson, Evan Durbin, Francis Edgeworth, Robert Giffen, Gottfried Haberler, Ralph Hawtrey, Friedrich Hayek, Eric Lindahl, Alfred Marshall, Gunnar Myrdal, Dennis Robertson, and Arthur Pigou. Indeed, as late as the early 1930s there was at least as much support among well-known economists for some kind of productivity norm as for the alternative of zero inflation. Even Keynes himself (1936, pp. 270-71) flirted with the idea (which, he noted, was more consistent with stability of money wages), only to reach a verdict favouring zero inflation.

Regrettably, the case for a productivity norm was all but forgotten in the aftermath of the 'Keynesian' revolution, which made price-level policy secondary to the goal of achieving 'full' employment. When monetarists once again made control of the price level a primary object of monetary policy, they did so by rehabilitating old arguments for a constant price level, leaving the productivity-norm alternative buried in obscurity.[9]

Today's proponents of zero inflation seldom grapple with the productivity-norm alternative.[10] Usually they just overlook

---

[9] See my (1995b) and (1996b) discussions of price-level policy in the history of economic thought. Milton Friedman's (1969) well-known argument for deflation as a means for achieving an 'optimum quantity of money' is distinct from earlier arguments for falling prices. As we shall see, it actually calls for deflation at a rate exceeding the rate of productivity growth.

Modern proposals for central bank targeting of nominal income (GNP or GDP) involve some of the same reasoning underlying earlier arguments for a productivity norm. Most proponents of income targeting are nonetheless zero inflationists, in that they regard it as a means of achieving a constant long-run price level.

[10] A noteworthy recent exception is Kevin Dowd (1995). See also my (1995a) reply.

it, as in treatments that pretend to argue for a constant price level when in fact merely arguing against secular inflation. Typical is *The Economist*'s statement (Anonymous, 1992, p. 11) that zero inflation is best 'because anything higher interferes with the ... ability [of prices] to provide information about relative scarcities'. The alternative of anything *lower* than zero, such as a price-level typically *falling* (but also occasionally rising) in response to changing productivity, is simply neglected.[11]

Zero inflationists' neglect of the alternative of secular deflation, along with their failure to consider the implications of productivity changes, has led them to embrace a faulty monetary policy ideal. In model economies where productivity does not change, it is relatively easy to make the case that zero inflation (that is, a constant price level) is consistent with keeping real economic activity on or close to its efficient and 'natural' path. But in reality productivity is constantly changing, generally for the better. In the real world, a little secular deflation, along with upward movements in the price level mirroring adverse supply shocks, would be *better* than zero inflation.

The Case for Zero Inflation

The idea that general macroeconomic stability requires stability of output prices probably predates the productivity norm alternative, being found in the writings of certain preclassical economists, including John Law. The need for stable prices was a recurrent theme of classical economics (see Viner, 1937, pp. 185-200, and Fisher, 1934) although, as noted earlier, many classical writers favoured a productivity norm. Arguments for a constant price level were, like arguments for a productivity norm, especially prominent in the decades just prior to the Keynesian revolution, with price-level stability

---

[11] Here and there the alternative of secular deflation is at least mentioned, but only to be immediately brushed aside on dubious pragmatic (rather than theoretical) grounds, e.g. 'because current policy debate centres on whether price stability should be the objective of monetary policy' (Carlstrom and Gavin, 1993, p. 9). Presumably the authors of this quote meant to say that debate centres on a choice between positive or zero inflation. Such pragmatism may have been justified several years ago, when few countries were even close to achieving zero inflation. Today it seems to be wholly out of place.

championed by Knut Wicksell, Gustav Cassel, Irving Fisher, John Maynard Keynes, Carl Snyder, and George Warren and Frank Pearson, among others. The Keynesian revolution made price-level policy play second fiddle to full employment until the monetarist counter-revolution – helped by worldwide outbreaks of inflation – brought the behaviour of the price level back to centre stage.[12]

The years since the monetarist counter-revolution have produced scores of academic briefs for zero inflation. One of the most eloquent, I think, was written by Leland Yeager a decade ago. According to Yeager (1986, p. 370), monetary disequilibrium – 'a discrepancy between actual and desired holdings of money at the prevailing price level' – causes deviations of employment and real output from their 'natural' or 'full-information' levels. A shortage of money at some given price level implies a corresponding surplus of goods, while a surplus of money implies a shortage of goods. Because a surplus of money eventually leads to higher prices, while a shortage of money eventually leads to lower prices, changes in the general level of prices ought to be regarded as 'symptoms or consequences' of monetary disequilibrium (Yeager, 1986, p. 373). It follows, according to Yeager, that a policy that adjusts the nominal money stock so as to avoid any need for movements in the general price level will avoid or reduce macro-economic disturbances. Such a policy requires that the quantity of money vary inversely with changes in money's velocity of circulation and directly with 'natural' changes in real output, *including changes in output stemming from changes in productivity.*[13]

Although it rests on a quantity theory of inflation and deflation, Yeager's argument for price-level stabilisation contradicts a naïve short-run interpretation of the quantity

---

[12] Although strict monetarists reject attempts to 'fine tune' the money supply, favouring monetary rules consistent with *long-run* price level stability only, many of their writings suggest that a *perfectly* constant price level would be ideal, if only human institutions could achieve it.

[13] Note that monetary policy is viewed here as being capable of reducing or eliminating monetary or 'unnatural' disturbances to real activity only. Policy cannot altogether 'stabilise' real activity in so far as 'natural' rates of output and employment are themselves subject to random change, as so-called 'real business cycle' theories suggest, and as I think is bound to be the case given the random nature of innovations to productivity.

theory: Yeager rejects the view, encountered in certain classical and New Classical writings, that changes in the stock of or demand for money can lead to instantaneous, uniform and transparent adjustments in all money prices, without altering patterns of production and consumption. Instead of subscribing to a naïve quantity theory, Yeager and other proponents of zero inflation insist that price-level adjustments generally 'do not and cannot occur promptly and completely enough to absorb the entire impact of [a] monetary change and so avoid quantity changes' (Yeager, 1986, p. 373).

Several obstacles stand in the way of instantly-equilibrating general price changes. First among them are fixed money contracts that cannot easily be 'indexed' to general price movements. Such contracts include both wage contracts and nominal debt contracts, the most notorious of which is the government's 'contract' offering holders of high-powered money balances a fixed, zero nominal rate of interest. Second, 'menu costs' and other expenses involved in posting and sometimes negotiating new money prices can make the price level 'sticky' in the short run.[14] Finally, sellers may be reluctant to change, and especially to lower, their prices in response to monetary disequilibrium even when the fixed costs of doing so are very small. Some analysts (e.g. Okun, 1980, pp. 145ff.) link this reluctance to the inelastic demand for products of firms whose customers face high shopping costs. Yeager (1986, p. 377) attributes it, in part at least, to the fact that money, 'unlike other goods, lacks a price and a market of its own'. This fact makes any equilibrating price level change something of a public good:

'Money's value (strictly, the reciprocal of its value) is the average of individual prices and wages determined on myriads of distinct though interconnecting markets for individual goods and services. Adjustment of money's value has to occur through supply and demand changes on these individual markets.'

---

[14] Although the 'New Keynesian' literature offers the most elaborate modern treatment of menu costs and other sources of nominal price rigidities (cf. Ball and Mankiw, 1994), awareness of such rigidities and their macro-economic implications pre-dates New Keynesian writings, and was in fact an integral part of 'old-fashioned monetarism'. On the relation between Old Monetarists and New Keynesians see Yeager (1996b).

Every affected transactor therefore regards the value of money 'as set beyond his control, except to the utterly trivial extent that the price he may be able to set on his own product arithmetically affects money's average purchasing power' (Yeager, 1986, p. 392). Why should a seller – especially one selling a good for which demand is inelastic – stick his neck out to correct a shortage of money by being the first in the market to lower his own product's price, when that seller might be better off letting others cut their prices first instead? New Keynesian writings also assign a crucial rôle to what they call 'aggregate demand externalities' as a source of sluggish price adjustment. According to Ball and Mankiw (1994, p. 18),

'The private and social gains from price adjustment [following a negative money shock] are very different. If a single firm adjusts its price, it does not change the position of its demand curve; it simply moves to a new point on the curve. This adjustment raises profits [not taking menu costs into account], but the gain is second order. In contrast, if *all* firms adjusted to the monetary shock, the aggregate price level would fall, real balances would return to their original level, and each firm's demand curve would shift back out. ... Unfortunately, an individual firm does not take this effect into account because, as a small part of the economy, it takes aggregate spending and hence the position of its demand curve as given. Thus firms may not bother to make price adjustments that, taken together, would end a recession.'[15]

The 'public' character of most of the benefits associated with a firm's adjusting its price in response to some monetary disequilibrium serves further to magnify the extent of price stickiness associated with any given 'menu' costs of price adjustment. The result is that, instead of appearing instantly following some monetary disturbance, a market-clearing general price level must be 'groped towards' by way of a 'decentralised, piecemeal, sequential, trial and error' process (Yeager, 1986, p. 375).

---

[15] New Keynesian writings treat this 'aggregate demand externality' argument as being applicable to imperfectly competitive markets only, on the ground that firms under perfect competition 'are price takers, not price setters' (Ball and Mankiw, 1994, p. 17). But, as Kenneth Arrow (1969) showed some time ago, under disequilibrium circumstances even firms that would otherwise be perfectly competitive become price setters.

17

Sluggish price adjustments are also likely to be uneven, with some prices adjusting ahead of others, so that equilibrating price-level movements typically involve temporary alterations of relative prices. Monetary theorists going as far back as Richard Cantillon and David Hume have understood that the relative price effects of any money supply shock depend on the monetary 'transmission mechanism' – that is, on the precise way in which nominal money balances are added to or subtracted from the economy. In fact, both money supply and demand shocks first make their presence felt, not in all markets at once, but in particular markets from which their effects slowly spread to the rest of the economy (Yeager, 1996a). Clark Warburton (an 'Old Monetarist') discusses the case of a positive money supply shock:

> 'The first change occurs at the point where the additional money is introduced into or taken out of the economy and is expressed in an increased or decreased demand for the goods and services desired by the persons directly affected by the change in the quantity of money.' ([1946] 1951, pp. 298-99)

Consider an unexpected round of central bank open-market purchases. The purchases 'inject' new high-powered money directly into the bond market, raising the value of government securities. The high-powered money quickly makes its way into commercial banks, who use it to make more loans, at lower rates.[16] Borrowers use the loans to purchase labour, capital goods, and durable consumer goods. Eventually an overall rise in spending raises the general price level, eliminating what had been a surplus of money balances. In principle, short-run monetary 'injection' effects can temporarily alter relative prices even if all money prices are quite flexible.

Temporary, relative price changes connected to bouts of monetary disequilibrium introduce 'noise' into money price signals, and thus 'degrade the information conveyed by individual prices' (*ibid.*, p. 374). Businessmen, workers and consumers rely on this degraded information (because it is better than nothing), and end up wasting resources. The

---

16 For evidence of this so-called 'liquidity effect' of money supply shocks on interest rates in the US see Lastrapes and Selgin (1995) and other references cited therein.

quote from *The Economist* (page 14 above) makes this very point. Monetary disturbances have real effects, not just because of the *time* it takes for the price level to adjust, but also because of the devious *path* taken by individual prices during the adjustment process.

Finally, changes in the overall price level of the sort needed to eliminate monetary disequilibrium can themselves promote 'unnatural' changes in real economic activity: economic actors may confuse general price changes with relative price changes, either because they suffer from 'money illusion' (a genuine failure to consider the meaning of general price changes) or because they only observe local price movements and infer (imperfectly) what is happening to prices in more far-removed markets. One frequently offered scenario of monetary expansion has workers reacting to higher money wage-rates while overlooking changes in the 'cost of living', so that employment rises (temporarily) above its natural or full-information level. Implicit in such scenarios is the assumption that changes in real money demand or nominal money supply, and consequent changes in the price level, are not perfectly anticipated by economic agents: while workers or consumers might easily anticipate steady, long-term trends in the equilibrium price level, they are likely to be surprised by, and fail to recognise, random changes. Nor would complete knowledge of the schedule of changes in the nominal money-stock (assuming such knowledge could be had) be sufficient to avoid price-level surprises, unless the public could also make precise forecasts of future changes in real money demand. It follows, then (according to zero inflationists), that the surest way to avoid money illusion is to avoid changes in the price level altogether.

Responding to the potential dangers of both monetary misperceptions and sluggish money price adjustment, advocates of zero inflation seek to *minimise the burden borne by the price system.* A policy of adjusting the nominal quantity of money whenever such an adjustment serves to keep the price level constant (but not otherwise) is supposed to do this both by reducing the number and size of needed adjustments in money prices, and by reducing the extent of temporary and unwarranted relative price changes (including altered real interest rates) arising in connection with any monetary disturbance.

19

The arguments considered so far have been arguments to the effect that zero inflation helps avoid short-run macro-economic disturbances. A separate but related argument for zero inflation claims it would eliminate long-run price-level uncertainty, thus making it easier for economising agents to rely on fixed money contracts, and debt contracts especially, without having to fear that those contracts will be undermined by unpredicted changes in the value of money. In principle, the efficiency of most fixed money contracts – the obvious exception being the zero nominal interest payment on cash – would not be undermined, even without resort to indexation, by some perfectly anticipated inflation or deflation: in this case optimal nominal payments can be determined *ex ante*, when contracts are first negotiated. Still, a randomly 'drifting' price level, such as a productivity norm would allow, is bound to be unpredictable and would, therefore (according to the standard view), be decidedly less conducive to long-run planning than a constant price level. Thus Robert F. Lucas (1990, pp. 77-8; emphasis added) asserts: 'If there is one thing about inflation that *all* economists can agree on, it is that a variable inflation generates the highest costs.'

I say, *not so fast.*

II. PRODUCTIVITY AND RELATIVE PRICES

There are two ways of gauging productivity, each suggesting a distinct kind of productivity norm. A *labour* productivity norm allows price-level changes that reflect changes in the ratio of real labour input to real output, while a *total factor* productivity norm allows price-level changes that reflect changes in the ratio of total real (labour and capital) inputs to total real output. An increase in total factor productivity tends, other things equal, to involve a proportional increase in labour productivity. But labour productivity also varies along with the capital intensity of production, with more or less capital-intensive methods yielding higher or lower levels of labour productivity. It follows, then, that a labour productivity norm and a total factor productivity norm yield the same results *if and only if capital intensity does not change.* For the time being, to simplify discussion, I will assume that this is indeed the case; that is, assume that changes in labour productivity are due exclusively to neutral changes in total factor productivity.[17] This allows me to discuss, in general terms, of the theoretical implications of 'a productivity norm' without bothering to distinguish between the two possible versions of such a norm. Later I will briefly consider pros and cons of the two alternatives in situations where they do in fact differ (pages 64-66).

Because the main purpose of this paper is to compare the theoretical implications of a productivity norm with those of zero inflation, the practical feasibility of both norms is taken for granted throughout most of the discussion that follows. To be precise, it is assumed that there is a fiat-money-issuing central monetary authority capable of insulating the price level from the effects of innovations to the velocity of money or real output. Under a zero inflation norm, the authority adjusts money growth in such a way as to offset the price-level effects of innovations to both velocity and real output,

---

[17] By a 'neutral' change in productivity I mean one that leaves both the degree of capital intensity and the price of capital services relative to that of labour unchanged.

21

including innovations to productivity. Under a productivity norm, the authority's response to innovations to the velocity of money and to the supply of factors of production are the same as under a zero inflation norm. But the authority does not respond to any change in productivity in so far as the change does not also involve a change in the velocity of money or the supply of factors of production. Of course, real-world monetary authorities are not so well-informed or well-behaved. Eventually I plan to acknowledge this fact, by proposing an institutional arrangement capable of automatically implementing something close to a productivity norm.

Underlying Tenets

The case for a productivity norm rests on many of the same tenets that underlie arguments for zero inflation. Both proposals take for granted the desirability of minimising the negative effects of monetary disequilibrium; both acknowledge the desirability, in theory, of accommodating changes in the velocity of money through opposite changes in its nominal quantity; and both reject attempts to employ monetary policy deliberately to divert the economy from its natural or full-information path.

The two norms also take for granted a belief that the public's expectations concerning the future state of macro-economic variables may be incorrect: people cannot be expected to form accurate forecasts of future movements in the price level or other macro-economic variables subject to random change. Both proposals assume that individuals prefer contracts fixed in money terms over contracts indexed to the price level or the supply of money. Finally, both proposals generally take for granted the presence of a monetary authority capable of adjusting the flow of nominal spending in response to supply or demand shocks in less time than it might take for the public to adjust prices and renegotiate contracts in response to the same shocks.[18]

There is, however, one tenet underlying arguments for zero inflation that must be rejected to make a case for a productivity norm. That is the view that, while changes in the

---

[18] There are exceptions. Dowd (1988, 1989) and Greenfield and Yeager (1983) propose 'laissez faire' schemes for stabilising the price level. On pages 67-69 I will suggest how a productivity norm might be (approximately) implemented without resort to a discretionary central bank.

relative prices of final goods always convey essential information to economic actors, changes in the *general* price level are always superfluous: they only serve as evidence of some prior monetary disequilibrium, which careful central bank management could have avoided, without conveying any new information about the state of the 'real economy' – of consumer preferences and production possibilities. In the words of Federal Reserve economist Robert Hetzel (1995, p.152), all changes in the price level, including changes connected to 'positive real sector shocks', merely provide 'evidence that the central bank is interfering with the working of the price system'. It follows, according to this view, that 'the information and scorekeeping functions of money would work best with no [general] change in prices. In that event, price tags would provide clear information about changes in relative prices' (Okun, 1980, p. 279; compare Jenkins, 1990, p. 21).

In reply, I plan to argue, first, that changes in the general price level *can* convey useful information to economic agents concerning the state of factor productivity and, second, that attempts to prevent price level movements from doing so themselves undermine the accuracy of price signals, diverting economic activity from its 'natural' course.

Superfluous and Meaningful Changes in the Price Level

Consider first an example of a genuinely superfluous change in the price level. Imagine an economy where both the supply of various factors of production and the productivity of those factors (and hence, real output or income) are unchanging. Imagine also that the real demand for various goods and services, apart from money, is unchanging. In such an economy, a change in the general level of output prices can occur only as a result of some change in the nominal quantity or velocity of money, leading to a change in the overall demand for final goods and services, that is, in aggregate spending or 'nominal income'. A central bank might, in principle at least, manage the stock of money so as to prevent such changes in nominal income, thereby keeping the price level constant. By assumption, consumer preferences and technology are not changing, so that the *only* information conveyed by any price level movement is information concerning the central bank's failure to maintain a stable value of nominal spending.

An analogy may help clarify the example. Imagine that you are listening to one of Bach's fugues for organ on the radio.

The signal is clear, but not too loud. All of a sudden the volume jumps up, then down, then up again, and so on. The changes in volume are superfluous at best: even if they do not alter a single note, they are certainly distracting, and they certainly are not an accurate and transparent reflection of what Bach intended. The only valuable information they convey is that some joker is messing with the remote control. In this analogy, individual notes are like individual relative price signals, and the loudness of the performance is like the general price level. Finally, changes in the 'volume' or flow of current through the radio are like changes in the flow of money through the economy.

But consider a somewhat different case. Suppose that, instead of playing a Baroque fugue for organ, which is supposed to be more-or-less equally loud from start to finish, the radio is playing a Tchaikovsky symphony. Now, even if no one touches the remote control, the loudness of the performance will vary substantially from movement to movement and even within individual movements. But these variations in loudness are far from being superfluous: they are an essential part of the score, fully intended by the composer. You would not want to try and eliminate them by toying with the volume level. On the contrary: a constant volume setting is still desirable, even though it no longer implies a (more or less) constant loudness level.

If an economy with constant productivity is like a Baroque organ fugue, an economy with changing productivity is more like a Romantic symphony. In the latter sort of economy, movements in the general price level may form a meaningful component of the 'tune' being played by money price signals: higher, 'louder' price signals can convey a message of fallen productivity and greater all-around scarcity (a higher price of output relative to inputs), while lower, 'softer' ones can convey a message of greater abundance (a lower price of output relative to inputs). Trying to improve an economy's performance by stabilising the price level in the face of changes in productivity is – I plan to argue – like trying to improve a symphony by adjusting the volume knob so that the majestic *finale* plays as softly as the sombre *adagio*.

To be clear: when productivity changes, so does the price of outputs relative to that of inputs. Such a relative price change ought to be reflected in the structure of money prices somehow, and *one way* of accomplishing this is to let the output price level change. Such changes in the price level are therefore *not* obviously superfluous. The question then becomes whether, all things considered, pertinent information concerning a change in productivity is best signalled by letting the output price level change, as a productivity norm would allow, or by changing *input* prices and nominal spending, as a norm of zero inflation would require. The 'radio' analogy suggests that the productivity norm is the better choice. But it is only an analogy, after all. The challenge is to show that changes in the 'volume' of spending are indeed a greater source of price-system distortions than volume-independent changes in the overall 'loudness' of money price signals.

The Productivity Norm and 'Menu' Costs

Let us first consider whether the overall burden of money price adjustments would be greater or smaller under a productivity-norm régime than under a zero-inflation régime. The régime that faces higher overall price adjustment or 'menu' costs will, presumably, be more prone to temporary relative price distortions.[19] One (admittedly simplistic) way to assess relative menu costs is to assume that all money prices are equally costly to adjust, and then count the absolute number of distinct money price changes needed to restore general equilibrium following an aggregate productivity shock in both a zero-inflation and a productivity-norm régime.[20]

Imagine an extreme case where a change in productivity affects the output of only one good. For such a case it is relatively easy to see, with the help of some rather heroic but analytically helpful assumptions, the advantages of a productivity norm. Suppose, for example, that 1,000 final goods are produced using three distinct factors of production.

---

[19] Following New Keynesian practice (e.g. Ball and Mankiw, 1994, p. 24), I use the term 'menu costs' metaphorically, to refer to both physical (direct) and managerial costs of changing prices.

[20] I am assuming that the lump-sum costs associated with a change in the price of a good do not depend on the number of units of that good being sold. This seems to be appropriate enough for prices listed in menus and catalogues; but not for genuine 'sticker' prices (like the ones I myself spent hours changing in a supermarket during the early 1970s). Electronic 'zebra stripe' readers are, however (to the immense relief of still-employed supermarket clerks everywhere), making the latter sort of price adjustment a thing of the past.

A technological improvement causes an outward shift in the supply schedule for good x, so that the quantity of good x producers would be willing to supply at any given price is twice the previous quantity. Suppose also that x formerly had a price (included in the price index) of one dollar per unit. Under a productivity norm policy, the monetary authorities do not adjust the quantity of money in response to a productivity shock, so that, with an unchanged velocity of money, nominal spending stays constant. Assuming (1) that x has a unitary price elasticity of demand; and (2) that demand for goods other than x is independent of real purchases of x (thus abstracting from the need for any 'secondary' relative-price adjustments), the price of x falls to 50 cents. This implies some (perhaps very slight) decline in the price level. Prices of all other goods remain unchanged, including the prices of the three factors of production whose marginal *value* productivity is also unchanged. The new equilibrium price structure requires one price adjustment only.

Now suppose, instead, that the price level is kept stable under identical circumstances. To accomplish this, the authorities expand the supply of money to achieve a uniform, though very slight, increase in the prices of 999 goods and of the three factors of production. The sole exception is good x, the price of which must (as in the previous case) still be allowed to fall, only less than in proportion with the improvement in its rate of output. Only in this way can the price index remain stable after allowing needed adjustments in relative prices.[21]

Going the next step, it is easy to generalise our conclusion by noting that it will hold for any possible set of productivity disturbances affecting less than all 1,000 goods. Thus, if the productivity of 999 of the 1,000 industries changes, then a productivity norm requires 999 individual money price adjustments, as opposed to 1,003 for a zero inflation norm.

---

[21] Some zero-inflationists might protest that their ideal policy would not require any monetary response to a single productivity-based price change, since such a change would typically have only a minuscule effect on the price level (*cf.* Dowd, 1995, p. 725n). But this stance begs the question: how many prices must be affected by underlying productivity shocks (or, alternatively, how great must be the overall impact of these shocks on a given price index) before price-stabilising policies come into play? Anyway, the argument being made here does not ultimately hinge on the assumption that output in one market only is altered by a change in productivity.

So does a productivity norm *always* involve fewer money price adjustments? The answer is no: retaining the same basic assumptions used above, it is possible to construct examples in which the number of money price adjustments required under a price-level stabilisation scheme is less than the number that would be required under the productivity norm. All of them would, however, involve some *perfectly uniform* percentage increase in productivity of all final-goods industries, such as would leave relative goods prices unchanged, requiring money price changes for factors of production only. Even here zero inflation would 'win' only provided that the number of distinct factors of production continued to be less than the number of distinct final goods.[22] In every other case, including ones in which all-around changes in productivity are combined with idiosyncratic changes involving one industry or group of industries, the total number of price changes required under zero inflation will always exceed the number required under a productivity norm, because a productivity norm generally requires fewer changes in nominal factor prices. Elsewhere I used the following example:

> 'Suppose that ten goods and three factors of production are initially priced at $8 each. Weighing all goods equally, let the initial price index have a value of $10(8) = 80$. Now suppose that output per unit input for one good quadruples, while output per unit of input for the rest doubles. Under the productivity norm, the price of the first good falls to 2; other goods prices fall to 4. [Factor prices don't change.] Ten money price changes are required in all, and the price index will assume a value of $9(4) + 2 = 38$. To achieve zero inflation, the money stock and input prices must increase by the factor 2.105; also, other prices must adjust to satisfy the formula $9(x) + x/2 = 80$, which implies $x = 8.421$. Therefore, the prices of nine goods must be increased from $8 to $8.421, while the price of the tenth good must fall to $4.21. The total number of price changes required under zero inflation thus exceeds the number required under a productivity norm by the number of distinctly-priced factors of production.' (Selgin, 1995a)

Because productivity, while constantly changing, never seems to advance uniformly in every sector of an economy

---

[22] Compare J. C. Gilbert (1955, p. 70), who reaches the same conclusion with regard, not to menu costs of price adjustment, but to distortions stemming from imperfect foresight.

(Kendrick and Grossman, 1980), it seems reasonable to conclude that, in practice, a productivity norm tends to involve fewer money-price adjustments than zero inflation. The 'menu' costs of price adjustment would therefore also be higher under zero inflation, assuming that they are lump-sum costs only. (As the example suggests, it makes no difference after all if the lump sum differs from one price to another.)[23]

Some readers may question the assumption that factor prices need not change under a productivity norm following idiosyncratic (for example, industry-specific) changes in productivity. They should bear in mind, though, that the supply of factors, and of labour especially, to any specific industry is highly elastic – a point recognised by at least one prominent zero-inflationist, the late Arthur Okun (1980, p. 98):

> 'Productivity is the key to real wage gains in the economy as a whole, but the differential growth of productivity across industries over time has only a limited effect on the wage structure, for obvious reasons. Workers in industries that, for technological reasons, have low productivity growth ... will quit in droves if they keep receiving [lower than average] wage gains. Conversely, firms in industries with rapid productivity growth do not need to pledge or deliver more rapid wage gains than others in order to hold on to their workers. Understandably, the differential growth of productivity across industries mainly changes relative prices over time ... rather than significantly altering the pattern of relative wages.'[24]

Okun's reasoning suggests that a productivity norm may have lower price-adjustment costs than zero inflation even if some of the 'heroic' assumptions made above are relaxed, that is, even allowing for the presence of secondary (income- and substitution-effect related) changes in relative output prices.

Suppose, for example, that a productivity shock leaves

---

[23] Allowing for *variable* as well as lump-sum costs of price adjustment *could* make a difference, since a productivity norm policy tends to involve fewer but larger price adjustments than its zero-inflation counterpart. It is, however, hard to see why costs of price adjustment should vary with the size of the adjustment to be made, especially in the case of output prices (the only ones that are likely to have to adjust substantially under a productivity norm).

[24] Okun's argument assumes that workers are reasonably free to move from job to job. See also Kendrick and Grossman (1980, p. 61).

equilibrium relative wage rates unchanged but has 'secondary' relative price effects so widespread as to require a change in the equilibrium relative price of every good. A price-level stability rule will require some adjustment to every money price, including money wage-rates. A productivity norm, in contrast, requires a change in the money price of every good, but (taking Okun's argument into account) does not require any change in money wage-rates. 'Menu' cost considerations therefore seem to offer clear grounds for preferring a productivity norm over zero inflation as a means for keeping the real economy on its 'natural' path.

Sellers' Reluctance to Lower Prices

Besides being relatively limited in number, the downward money-price adjustments that must occur under a productivity norm in response to some innovation to productivity are also relatively easy and painless compared to adjustments required (under identical circumstances) to maintain a constant price level. This means that we should reconsider the initial, tacit assumption that the 'menu' cost of changing a money price does not depend on the nature of the innovation necessitating the change. Money-price changes are likely to cost less when they are connected to productivity changes because productivity changes often imply changes in unit production costs.[25] A decline in the selling price of some product for which demand is unit elastic, reflecting a drop in the product's real unit cost of production and consequent outward shift in its supply schedule, leaves producers' revenues and profits unaffected. Such a change need not place producers under any pressure to negotiate new wage-rates and salaries or even to change the size of their workforce. Because the reduction of prices required here is 'painless' – a mere result of having more to sell – there is no reason for producers to resist it or to act as if the benefits from not resisting it were mainly 'public' ones, external to themselves.

Likewise, for producers to increase prices in the face of shrunken productivity is relatively painless compared to what they must do if the monetary authorities insist on counteracting the rise in prices. Ralph Hawtrey (1930, p. 79)

---

[25] Changes in *total factor* productivity imply like changes in unit production costs. This is not always the case for changes in *labour* productivity.

once offered the following illustration, where 'consumers' outlay' is another name for total spending or nominal income:

'Suppose...that a consumers' outlay of £100,000,000 has been applied to 100,000,000 units of goods, and that producers who have hitherto received £20,000,000 for 20,000,000 units find their output reduced to 10,000,000 units, but the price of their product doubled. They still receive £20,000,000 and the other producers can continue to receive £80,000,000 for 80,000,000 units. But as £100,000,000 is now spent on 90,000,000 units the price level has risen by one-ninth. In order to counteract that rise, the consumer's outlay must be reduced from £100,000,000 to £90,000,000. Every group of producers will find the total proceeds of its sales reduced by 10 per cent. Wages, profits and prices will be thrown out of proportion, and every industry will have to face the adverse effects of flagging demand and falling prices. The producers whose prices have been raised by scarcity will be no exception. Their total receipts are reduced in the same proportion, and they must reduce wages like their neighbours.'

Hawtrey also showed that his argument does not depend on the assumption of a unitary elasticity of demand:

'If the shortage is in a product of which the elasticity is greater than unity, the adverse effect on the producers of that product is greater and on the other producers less. If elasticity is less than unity the adverse effect on the former is less and may be more than counteracted, but what they gain their neighbours lose. Whatever the circumstances, the stabilisation of the commodity price level in face of scarcity[26] will always tend to cause depression.'

The claim that it is relatively easy for producers to adjust prices in response to supply shocks agrees with many theories of output price rigidity. These theories suggest that product prices will be rigid only to the extent that factor prices are rigid, because product prices are often set according to 'implicit contracts' promising some fixed percentage mark-up of prices above unit costs (Okun, 1980, p. 170). Although this view accounts for a sluggish adjustment of product prices in response to changes in nominal income, it does not predict any ill-adjustment in situations of changing productivity. In

---

[26] Hawtrey should have said *unexpected* scarcity.

the latter case, unit costs of production are themselves changing, so that adjustments in product prices tend to take place, even as factor prices and the total outlay for factors stay the same, to preserve a constant mark-up. Empirical studies broadly support this conclusion, by revealing that output prices are in fact 'much more responsive to changes in costs than to shifts in demand' (*ibid.*, p. 169). It follows, as at least one zero-inflationist (Arthur Okun again) has admitted, that where 'implicit contracts ... are especially important, there may be a case for a horizontal wage trend (and a corresponding negative trend in prices)' (*ibid.*, p. 280).[27]

Up to now we have granted zero inflationists' assumption that random changes in equilibrium money prices are entirely unanticipated by economic agents. This assumption is, however, not really appropriate in the case of downward price adjustments associated with changes in productivity. In truth such adjustments are likely to be *perfectly* anticipated *by price-setting agents in the directly affected markets*. The reason is simple: improvements in productivity are often (if not always) consciously aimed at by producers, who seek them precisely because they want to sell more than their rivals by charging less, without sacrificing profits (Haberler, 1931, p. 20).[28] That downward equilibrium price movements associated with improvements in productivity are (unlike ones associated with a collapse in spending) often expected by producers gives us further grounds for thinking that they will not be resisted by

---

[27] Okun's reasons for ultimately advocating zero inflation rather than a productivity norm are worth noting, especially in light of his own reliance upon an implicit-contracts model of aggregate unemployment. His reasons are (1) that a shift from zero inflation to deflation 'would sacrifice some output for a period of time' and (2) that a 'modest upward trend in wage rates' would allow for occasional changes in relative wages without requiring as many cuts in nominal wages as a productivity norm would require. Okun's stand illustrates the difficulty proponents of zero inflation have in rejecting a productivity norm without implying that some *positive* inflation rate would be advantageous. Why assume that the transition costs of going from zero inflation to, say, 2 per cent deflation will be any greater than those of going from 12 per cent (the approximate US rate when Okun's book appeared) to zero? And, if a 'modest' upward trend in wages (consistent with zero inflation) requires fewer nominal wage cuts, then a less modest trend, consistent with positive inflation, requires still fewer.

[28] Naturally this cannot be said concerning *setbacks* to productivity, which are generally unexpected.

those producers and that they will, therefore, rapidly translate into an equilibrating change in the general price level.

Monetary Injection Effects

Yet another difference between price adjustments made necessary by unaccommodated changes in productivity and adjustments made necessary by changes in the flow of nominal income (as must occur if the price level is to be kept stable in the face of productivity changes) is that the former come about in a relatively direct manner.

A productivity change implies an immediate shift in output supply schedules and market-clearing prices (with no necessary change in input supply schedules) for those products being produced more or less efficiently than before. In contrast, as we have seen, a less-than-perfectly anticipated change in the money stock, such as would be needed to maintain a stable price level in the face of some unanticipated but persistent change in aggregate productivity, affects most prices only indirectly, through a sequence of shifts in nominal demand schedules beginning with schedules in a few markets only – bond markets, usually – and eventually spreading through the rest. Relative prices, including real interest rates, are thus displaced from their natural or full-information values. It follows that, instead of avoiding monetary 'injection effects', a consistent policy of price-level stabilisation is likely to be a source of such effects whenever aggregate productivity changes unpredictably.

Yeager (1996a) disagrees with this view. He argues that, because any increase in productivity will typically be accompanied by an increased demand for real money balances, a monetary expansion aimed at stabilising the price level as productivity advances only serves to accommodate the public's demand for 'increased intermediation services', avoiding a temporary excess demand for money and associated break in the flow of spending. This supposedly helps to avoid loan-market 'liquidity effects', keeping real interest rates at their natural levels.

But Yeager overlooks the rapid, if not immediate, tendency of output prices to respond to productivity (that is, unit cost) changes. He overlooks, in other words, how changes in the demand for real money balances based on innovations to

32

aggregate productivity are accommodated by falling prices automatically and *well ahead of any possible monetary policy response.*

Because nominal prices do *not* adjust sluggishly to productivity (as opposed to aggregate spending) shocks, no excess demand for money arises. The flows of spending and intermediation continue unimpeded. Attempts by a monetary authority to 'accommodate' an increased demand for real balances based on some concurrent change in productivity do not, therefore, actually serve to offset prior shortages of money at all. Instead, such attempts disturb established states of monetary equilibrium by reversing or 'rolling back' prior, equilibrating changes in money prices. The process of 'rolling back' the price level itself introduces excess liquidity into the economy, pushing real interest rates temporarily below their natural levels.

Monetary Misperceptions

Despite being both 'automatic' and frequently anticipated by those who undertake them, price adjustments linked to productivity shocks will nonetheless be widely unexpected. This raises the question of whether price adjustments, insofar as they involve changes in the price level, might inspire 'money illusion' or more subtle money price 'signal-extraction' problems – causes of distortions to real activity that could operate even if prices and wages were perfectly flexible.[29] But an unexpected change in the price level linked to some opposite, unexpected change in productivity is not just extra 'noise' added to underlying relative price signals. The price-level change constitutes a meaningful signal that overall unit production costs are changing. Instead of tricking people into making wrong decisions, price-level movements of this sort actually help to avoid economic waste.

In contrast, if the monetary authorities prevent the price level from changing along with a change in productivity (for example, by making more units of money available just as expanded outputs reach retailers' shelves), *their* actions *will* add 'static' to the price system, by causing a general change in aggregate spending. To be sure, agents will not be 'surprised'

---

[29] By 'perfectly flexible' I mean free of menu costs and other adjustment impediments.

in this case by any change in the overall level of output prices; but they *will* be surprised by a general outward shift in both output and input demand schedules. Although the price level does not change, agents may confuse this general, *nominal* increase in demand with changes in the real demand for particular goods and factors of production.

Formally, the argument here is essentially the same one found in many recent proposals and assessments of nominal income (GNP or GDP) targeting.[30] The argument can be illustrated using the aggregate supply-demand framework shown in Figure 2a. The illustration includes both a long-run (LAS) and a short-run (SAS) aggregate supply schedule, where the former is vertical and the latter allows for the possibility of short-run monetary misperceptions and is therefore upward-sloping.[31] The rectangular-hyperbola, unit-elastic aggregate demand (AD) schedule shows all combinations of the price level (P) and real output (y) consistent with some given level of spending, which is assumed to be controllable by the monetary authorities. Real output starts out at some 'natural'

---

[30] See, among others, Bean (1983), Bradley and Jansen (1989), Frankel and Chinn (1995), Haraf (1986), and McCallum (1987, 1995).

[31] Although zero-inflationists will generally accept the assumption of a vertical long-run supply schedule (and associated vertical Phillips Curve), others reject it. For example, in a recent, influential article George Akerlof, William Dickins, and George Perry (1996) appeal to downward nominal wage rigidities to argue for a curving Phillips Curve. Here, a positive rate of inflation is supposedly needed to achieve maximum employment. The argument, in essence, is that, even assuming a non-negative trend for the *average* level of money wage-rates (as would exist under a productivity norm), changes in the distribution of the demand for labour across industries would necessitate downward money wage adjustments in adversely affected industries to allow them to maintain their workforce. If money wages are rigid downwards, workers in these industries will become unemployed.

This framework appears to exaggerate the extent to which money wage adjustments are needed to achieve an efficient allocation of labour in response to both temporary and permanent shifts in the distribution of the demand for labour. In the case of merely temporary shifts, employers may continue to employ the same number of workers, at their original wage-rates, knowing (or believing) that better days are ahead, and wanting to preserve good-will. In the case of permanent shifts in demand, lay-offs can perform the same allocative rôle as money wage-rate cuts – inducing workers to seek employment in industries where demand has risen. In the former case, inflation is not needed to avoid unemployment; in the latter, inflation could at best avoid unemployment only by perpetuating an inefficient allocation of labour.

level $y(n)$, consistent with the intersection, at point $a(n)$, of the short-run aggregate supply, long-run aggregate supply and aggregate demand schedules.

Figure 2b is the corresponding labour-market diagram, where w is the money wage-rate, and N stands for man-hours of employment. The nominal demand for labour (LD) is assumed (for simplicity's sake) to reflect the state of aggregate demand, while long- and short-run labour supply schedules (LLS and SLS, respectively) hold up their aggregate supply counterparts. Allowing that productivity is subject to change, the vertical LLS schedule implies that labour supply is inelastic in the long run with respect to changes in real wage-rates. In the short run, however, workers may engage in some 'intertemporal substitution' of labour for leisure or *vice-versa*, for example, by working less today with the intention of working more tomorrow in response to a perceived decline in their real wage-rates that they believe might be temporary. The upward-sloping SLS schedule allows for such an intertemporal substitution effect based on monetary misperceptions: workers perceive changes in their money wage-rates at once, while perceiving changes in the price level only after some delay. Workers therefore temporarily *mis*perceive their real wage-rates.

The framework here, unlike the one implicit in the earlier discussion, does not invoke 'menu' costs of price adjustment. In reality, of course, menu costs and monetary misperception effects may simultaneously provide the basis for non-neutral effects of changes in the supply of or demand for money. At the moment, however, I wish to allow for monetary misperception effects only, abstracting from menu costs. The price-level policy best suited for avoiding monetary misperception effects may, after all, differ from the policy best suited for minimising menu costs.

Now consider the effect of a decline in spending, from AD to AD^1, due, say, to an unexpected fall in the velocity of money. The natural rate of output has not changed, but with less being spent, the nominal demand for labour declines. Because workers are unaware of an ensuing drop in prices, the economy moves along the short-run aggregate and labour supply schedules to point b, involving a below-natural level of employment and output and lowered wage and price levels.

Figure 2: A Negative Demand Shock

a. The Output Market

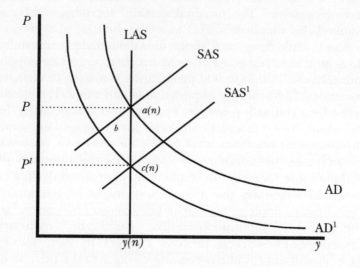

b. The Labour Market

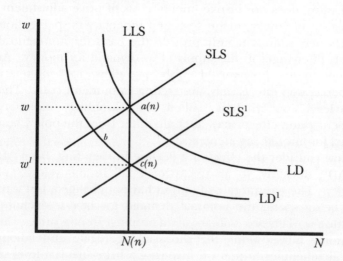

Eventually, the misperception effect wears off – an event signified by a downward shift in the short-run labour and aggregate supply schedules, from SLS to SLS[1] and from SAS to SAS[1]. The new short-run aggregate supply schedule crosses the new aggregate demand schedule at a point, $c(n)$, that is once again consistent with natural levels of output and employment.

The policy implication of the above example ought to be straightforward: assuming they have the power to do so, the monetary authorities should make sure that aggregate demand does not fall, by offsetting any tendency for velocity to shrink with some appropriate increase in the money stock.

Next, consider the effects of a positive productivity shock, starting with the same initial equilibrium as in the previous example. This case is illustrated in Figure 3. Assume that the monetary authority sticks to a productivity norm, and so does nothing (assuming a fixed 'natural' rate of factor input) other than maintain a stable level of aggregate spending. In this case, unit production costs fall, meaning that more output is produced by the same quantity of labour and capital. Both the long-run and the short-run aggregate supply schedules shift to the right, from SAS to SAS[1] and from LAS to LAS[1], and so does the natural rate of output. The resulting 'natural' equilibrium, $d(n)$, involves the same lowering of the price level as the previous case, but no change in money wage-rates (since neither the supply schedule nor the demand schedule for labour shifts), hence, no monetary misperception effects. Although workers may still fail to perceive or respond to the general decline in prices, the 'failure' turns out to be optimal: the short-run increase in *real* wage-rates is consistent with long-run equilibrium. Output moves directly to its new natural rate, $y(n)[1]$.

What happens in the case just described if the authorities, instead of stabilising spending, attempt to stabilise the price level? Then, rather than let the economy come to rest at its 'natural' equilibrium, $d(n)$, the authorities expand the money stock to generate a higher aggregate demand schedule (AD[1]) that intersects the new long-run supply schedule at a point consistent with the old price level. This expansion of spending *raises* the demand for labour to LD[1], and so causes the economy to 'ride up' its new, short-run labour and aggregate supply schedules to equilibrium points (*e*) involving

Figure 3: A Positive Productivity Shock

a. The Output Market

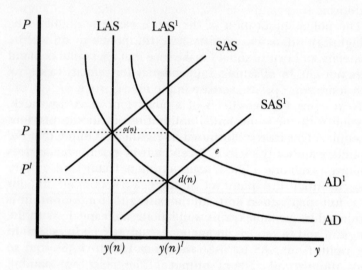

b. The Labour Market

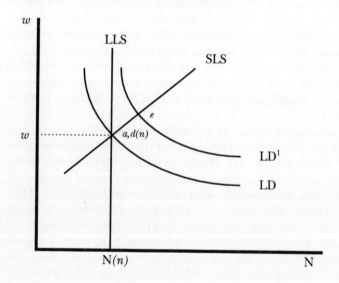

higher-than-natural levels of employment and output. As in the case of a pure spending shock, things return to normal once the short-run aggregate supply schedule adjusts. Thus, attempts to stabilise the price level in the face of productivity shocks themselves become a source of disequilibrating monetary misperception effects that would be avoided if the price level were simply allowed to adjust along with changing unit production costs.

Figure 4 shows what happens if the monetary authorities take steps to prevent an *increase* in the price level following a *set-back* to productivity. The adjustments are opposite to those just described. To combat the tendency of prices to rise, the authorities must reduce the money stock and aggregate demand. As was the case in the first illustration (where demand fell but productivity was unchanged), the decline in spending diverts the economy to a set of equilibrium points (*g*) involving below-natural levels of employment and output. Indeed, from the point of view of workers, who initially perceive a nominal shift in the demand for labour only without noticing any similar shift in the demand for output, the two situations are identical. Evidently, it is shifts in aggregate demand, and not changes in the price level *per se*, that sponsor monetary misperceptions and consequent, 'unnatural' changes in output and employment.

What are we to make, then, of the conventional linking of monetary misperception problems to price-level movements? The convention is merely an unfortunate byproduct of economists' habit of ignoring (and of constructing models that routinely exclude) changes in productivity. This habit leads them wrongly to identify changes in the price level with changes in aggregate spending. From here it is but a short step to the (false) conclusion that unexpected movements in the price level should be positively correlated with cyclical movements in output. The truth is rather that output may be either positively or negatively related to 'price surprises', depending on whether the surprises reflect unexpected shifts in aggregate demand or shifts in aggregate supply. That theorists should find little overall correlation between cyclical variations in real output and unexpected changes in the price level is therefore neither surprising nor necessarily inconsistent with a monetary interpretation of the business cycle.

Figure 4: A Negative Productivity Shock

a. The Output Market

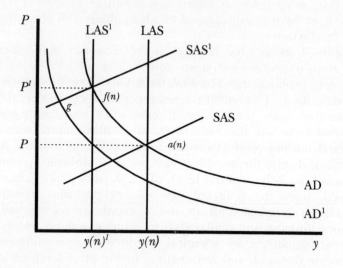

b. The Labour Market

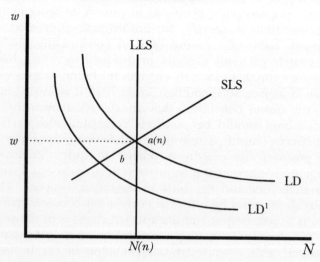

III. DEBTORS AND CREDITORS

Price Movements and 'Windfalls'

For separate consideration is the effect of a productivity norm on contracts between debtors and creditors, where debtors have committed themselves to making fixed-money payments in the future, and creditors have agreed to receive these fixed-money payments.[32] It is generally assumed that fixed nominal debt contracts are easier to write and execute than other kinds, including contracts in which payments are indexed to some measure of the general price level. Proponents of zero inflation claim the absence of unexpected price-level changes to be a requirement for the successful employment of such fixed-debt contracts, and especially for avoiding 'windfall' transfers of wealth from creditors to debtors or *vice-versa*. So long as the price-level is kept constant, the argument goes, neither debtors nor creditors will (on the whole) have any reason to regret their reliance upon fixed-debt contracts. A constant price level is also supposed to promote long-term investment by eliminating a source of uncertainty that would otherwise discourage such investment (e.g. Hoskins, 1990, p.35).

The argument, like most arguments for a constant price level, is perfectly valid so long as aggregate productivity is unchanging. But if productivity is subject to random changes, the argument no longer applies. Imagine, for example, that everyone expects both the price level and productivity to remain unchanged.[33] Then, if the price level is kept constant in the face of unexpected improvements in productivity, readily adjusted money incomes, including profits, dividends,

---

[32] Although the discussion that follows refers explicitly to loan contracts, most of the same considerations apply to other fixed-money obligations, including explicit or implicit fixed-money wage contracts.

[33] The argument that follows still holds if we allow that agents accurately anticipate *some* changes in productivity, while also anticipating how the monetary authorities will respond to these changes.

and some wage payments, will increase; and recipients of these flexible money payments will benefit from the improvements in real output. Creditors, however, will not be allowed to reap any gains from the same improvements, as debtors' real interest payments will not increase despite a general improvement in real earnings. Although an unchanged price level does fulfil creditors' price-level expectations, creditors may still regret having engaged in fixed nominal contracts, rightly sensing that they have missed out on their share of an all-around advance of real earnings, which share they might have been able to insist upon had they (and debtors also) known about the improvement in productivity in advance.

Now imagine instead that the price level is allowed to fall in response to improvements in productivity. Creditors will automatically enjoy a share of the improvements, while debtors will have no reason to complain: although the real value of the debtors' obligations does rise, so does their real income, while the *nominal* payments burden borne by debtors is unchanged. Debtors can, in other words, *afford* to pay higher real rates of interest; they might therefore, for all we know, have been quite happy to agree to the same fixed nominal interest rate had both they and creditors been equipped with perfect foresight.[34] Therefore the debtors' only possible cause for regretting the (unexpected) drop in prices is their missed opportunity to benefit from an alternative (zero inflation) that would in this case have given them an artificial *advantage* over creditors. The debtors 'loss' is, as Haberler (1931, p. 21) put it, only *lucrum cessans*, not *damnum emergens*.

Many years ago Samuel Bailey (1837, pp. 115-18) made much the same point. Suppose, he said, that A lends £100 to B for one year, and that prices in the meantime unexpectedly fall 50 per cent. If the fall in prices is due to a decline in spending, A obtains a real advantage, while B suffers an equivalent loss. But if the fall in prices is due to a general improvement in productivity, A's gain is not matched by any absolute diminution of B's wealth, because the enhanced real value of B's repayment corresponds with the enhanced ease with which B and other members of the community are able to produce a given amount of real wealth. Likewise, if the price

---

[34] Dowd (1995, p. 720) seems to miss the point here in insisting that 'one cannot say that the price-level fall does not matter to [the average debtor] because his real income was rising anyway'.

level were allowed to rise unexpectedly because of a halving of productivity, 'both A and B would lose nearly half the efficiency of their incomes', but 'this loss would arise from the diminution of productive power, and not from the transfer of any advantage from one to the other'. Bailey concluded from this that productivity-based price level changes offer 'no pretext for interfering with the literal construction of [a fixed-money] contract, as a contract for quantity without reference to value' (*ibid.*, p. 121). By the same token, the price change would not justify an attempt by the monetary authorities to interfere with the course of prices.

Still another way to think of the argument is in terms of optimal indexation. The usual view is that, absent costs of doing so, debtors and creditors would be inclined to index money rates of interest to the rate of inflation or deflation, so that more inflation means higher (nominal) interest rates *ex post*, and more deflation means lower (nominal) interest rates. But if the growth rate of productivity (hence, real income) is also subject to shocks, debtors and creditors might be just as anxious to index money rates of interest to the rate of productivity growth, so that slower productivity growth leads to lower (real) interest rates *ex post* and more rapid productivity growth leads to higher (real) interest rates.[35] Under a productivity norm, the price level and productivity move opposite to one another, so that the two forms of indexation would have offsetting effects, making both redundant. Under zero inflation, in contrast, productivity indexing would require an upward adjustment of nominal interest rates proportional to the higher growth rate of real (and, in this case, nominal) income.

If the debtor-creditor advantages of price-level stability are not obvious in situations where productivity is advancing, they are still less obvious in situations where productivity suffers a setback. Francis Edgeworth (1925 [1889], p. 222) once observed that those who plead for stabilising the money value of nominal debts in times of increasing prosperity 'might be embarrassed if the principle were extended to the case of

---

[35] Irving Fisher is usually credited with noting that, other things being equal, the lower the rate of inflation, the lower the full-information money rate of interest. But Fisher (1930, pp. 383-84) also observed that 'other things being equal...when in any community the [real] income streams of its inhabitants are increasing, the [real] rate of interest will be high'.

declining prosperity'. As Dennis Robertson (1922, p. 121) put it, quoting Shylock:

> "'I'll have my bond, speak not against my bond" – is that a plea which should be listened to from a debenture-holder or Trade Unionist in a country shivering for lack of fuel or impoverished by chronic warfare?'

Indeed, if productivity unexpectedly falls – as it may during wartime or when a harvest fails or when a cartel manages to restrict output of some basic raw material – the unfortunate consequences, both ethical and practical, of a price-level stabilisation rule cannot easily be denied, for the rule here requires a *contraction* of all non-fixed money incomes. Besides leading to a further depression of real activity (if prices and wages are sticky), such a rule might well result in certain debts not being paid at all. Some creditors might, in other words, escape the consequences of fallen productivity, by letting others bear a disproportional burden. Is such an outcome *more* equitable than one that causes all creditors to suffer some loss? Does it enhance the performance of fixed contracts, or otherwise encourage long-term investment? Surely not.

Some may say this conclusion is unscientific – that it rests on the arbitrary ethical premise that creditors 'deserve' a share of general improvements in as well as general setbacks to productivity. Kevin Dowd (1995, p. 720), for one, wonders 'what is attractive about it?' Indeed, some may hold to an entirely different ethical premise, sharing, for instance, Keynes's view (1936, p. 271) that denying the 'rentier' any share of productivity gains has the 'social advantage of ... diminishing the burden of debt'. It would seem that considerations of equity alone cannot provide any basis for choosing between a productivity norm and a stable price level.

There is something to such arguments. Economists should not smuggle ethical judgements into what purports to be a discussion of positive requirements for an efficient use of resources; and they should not recommend a reform of monetary policy aimed solely at altering the distribution of 'gains and losses from good and bad foresight' (Yeager, 1992, p. 60). As Robert F. Lucas (1990, p. 76) rightly observes,

> '[a]n economist has no comparative advantage in discussing redistribution, for there is nothing in his tool kit to enable him to make objective, interpersonal comparisons between winners and losers'.

But I am not merely claiming that a productivity norm leads to a more equitable distribution of wealth than zero inflation. I am claiming as well that it keeps us closer to a full-information ideal, with realised real rates of interest generally remaining near their perfect-foresight counterparts. Perhaps insisting upon a full-information ideal for debtor-creditor earnings itself involves some smuggling-in of ethics, or an attempt to 'second-guess parties to voluntary contracts' (Yeager, 1992, p. 60). But if so, zero inflationists can take no comfort from the fact, since it undermines all monetary policy arguments, including their own, that take for granted the desirability of minimising departures of real output and employment from their 'natural' levels.

In so far as it suggests that a *variable* inflation rate can actually help achieve a full-information ideal for resource allocation, my argument also contradicts the claim that a variable inflation rate is the worst kind as well as the claim that an uncertain price level 'causes agents to make more [*sic*] mistakes they would otherwise have avoided, and thus ... to have more regrets later on' (Dowd, 1995, p. 722; *cf.* Buchanan, 1962). The truth is rather that an unvarying and hence 'certain' price level may itself be a source of regret to economic agents if it remains unvarying despite fluctuations in productivity.

I therefore reject the argument that monetary policy ought to aim at avoiding unpredictable changes in the price level. Using monetary policy to stabilise the price level is not at all like making the weather more predictable, as James Buchanan and Kevin Dowd have claimed (*ibid.*). Stabilising the price level is more like making *barometric readings* (nominal indicators of meteorological conditions) predictable, while leaving the weather itself as uncertain as ever: price level movements allowed under a productivity norm are merely nominal indicators of underlying changes in productivity. Just as it is desirable for barometer readings to be unpredictable if the weather itself changes randomly, it is desirable for the price level – a useful 'barometer' of changing unit costs – to be unpredictable to the extent that aggregate productivity changes randomly.

The Productivity Norm and the Optimum Quantity of Money

The most well-understood welfare cost of inflation stems from its ability to act as a tax on high-powered cash holdings:

because cash usually bears a fixed nominal interest return of zero, any positive rate of inflation implies a negative pecuniary return on cash, where money-holders' losses are money-issuers' gains.[36] Because its burden is felt in proportion to base money holding, inflation, to the extent that it is anticipated, encourages people to hold a less than 'optimal' real quantity of money and to incur correspondingly high transactions costs of exchange. This reduction of equilibrium money balances might actually aggravate the business cycle, by reducing the extent of monetary 'buffer stocks' that serve to insulate aggregate nominal income from disruptions to the flow of spending in particular markets (Leijonhufvud, 1981, Chapter 6).

So positive inflation injures money holders. But so does zero inflation. As Milton Friedman (1969) pointed out in a now-famous article, what is really needed to induce people to hold an 'optimum quantity of money' is, not zero inflation, but *deflation* at a rate equal to the real rate of interest on riskless short-term bonds.[37] A productivity norm, by allowing the price level to decline secularly as productivity grows, comes closer to Friedman's formula than price-level stabilisation, and to this extent does a better job than zero inflation of minimising the 'tax' on money. Still, a productivity norm can never actually achieve Friedman's ideal.

The reasons for both conclusions can best be made clear through an illustration.[38] Imagine an economy with a capital stock made up entirely of maintenance-free machines, each producing £500 of output annually and initially selling for £10,000 (implying a discount rate of 5 per cent). In equilibrium, an investment in fixed-value bonds earns the

---

[36] In most banking systems bank reserves are also non-interest-bearing, so that bank deposits are also 'taxed' by inflation, albeit (given fractional reserve ratios) at a lower rate than cash.

[37] As Friedman himself recognised, an optimum quantity of money might be achieved without deflation by having all forms of money, including cash, bear nominal interest. A move to 'free banking' (as discussed below, pp.67-69) would certainly take us in this direction. Nevertheless, it seems likely that some form of paper currency – whether government or private – will continue to remain in use for some time. White (1987) argues that the costs of paying nominal interest on such currency are, even under competitive conditions, likely to be prohibitive.

[38] The illustration draws on similar ones presented in Gilbert (1957).

same real rate of return as an investment in machines. Suppose that money incomes, the price level, and productivity in this economy are, initially, constant. Bonds then earn both a money and a real rate of return of 5 per cent, while money earns a rate of return of zero.

Next, imagine that, holding the stock of machines constant, regular design changes cause their physical productivity to increase at an annual rate of 4 per cent.[39] Under a productivity norm, the output price level declines at a rate of 4 per cent, and money earns an equivalent real rate of return. Although both the monetary value of output and the rental price of machines remain unchanged, the real return on machines also increases by 4 percentage points. An investment in machines therefore earns a real return of 9·2 per cent.[40] It follows that *the money rate of interest on fixed-nominal-value bonds will continue to be 5 per cent*, making their real return the same as that of a machine. There is still a 5 percentage-point gap between the real return on bonds and the real return on money.

Now suppose that the authorities decide to stabilise the price level. To do this they must engineer a 4 per cent annual growth rate of money earnings. The prices of factors of production will then increase at the same rate, so that capital continues to earn a real return of 9·2 per cent. The equilibrium money rate of interest on bonds will then rise to 9·2 per cent, making for a 9·2 percentage-point gap between the rate of return on bonds and that on money. Equilibrium money holdings therefore decline, moving the economy further from Friedman's ideal.

The above illustration makes it equally clear, however, that *a productivity norm itself can never suffice to generate an 'optimum' quantity of money in Friedman's sense.*[41] The achievement of Friedman's ideal requires, not merely deflation mirroring the rate of productivity growth, but deflation at a rate *exceeding* the

---

[39] Although the supply of any one kind of machine is likely to be highly elastic with respect to a change in that machine's relative productivity, the supply of machines-in-general – that is, the supply of capital – may be quite inelastic with respect to a change in machines' overall productivity.

[40] $(1·05)(1·04) = 1·092$

[41] Nor, by the same token, is a productivity norm policy ever likely to give rise to negative equilibrium money rates of interest, as some fear it might.

rate of growth of productivity, that is, deflation brought about in part at least by a reduction in the money earnings of labour and capital. It seems unlikely that the benefits of such a policy (larger equilibrium money holdings) would be worth the costs (disruptions associated with the downward rigidities in factor prices).[42]

---

[42] According to S. C. Tsiang (1969, p. 273), Friedman's ideal, viewed as a policy recommendation, 'goes wrong [in regarding] aggregate utility...as merely the sum total of the utility which individual holders of money balances might be expected to derive from their own holdings. The truth is, however, that...when the real balances of the whole economy are increased together, there would arise considerable diseconomies to the economy [involving] the gradual breakdown of the stability of the price system and the impairment of the efficiency of the financial market in channelling savings toward investment. Moreover, these diseconomies would begin to appear long before we reach the so-called optimal state of complete satiation of the demand for real money balances'. Friedman himself did not present his theoretical ideal as a practical policy recommendation.

IV. HISTORICAL IMPLICATIONS OF THE PRODUCTIVITY NORM

Theoretical arguments favouring a productivity norm run counter to macro-economic conventional wisdom in a number of obvious ways. They suggest that a falling price level is not necessarily a sign or source of depression, that a rising price level is not necessarily a sign of excessive monetary expansion nor a justification for monetary tightening, and that a stable price level is not necessarily conducive to macro-economic stability. Modern economic history is filled with episodes supporting each of these claims, while contradicting conventional thinking as embodied in arguments for zero inflation. The following are a few examples.

The 'Great Depression' of 1873-1896

The period from 1873 to 1896 bothered economic historians for decades.[43] Both people living at the time, and many later academics, branded it a time of unprecedented economic stagnation throughout the gold-standard nations. In Britain (supposedly the hardest hit), 'there was an overwhelming mass of opinion – in reports of parliamentary committees and royal commissions, in parliamentary debates, newspapers, books, pamphlets, and speeches – that conditions were bad' (Musson, 1959, p. 199).

The popular impression was supported by a single, indisputable fact: Britain and most of the West had witnessed a 'uniquely persistent deflation' (Landes, 1965, p. 462) with the British wholesale price index losing close to one-third of its value in less than a quarter-century. For many this 'most drastic deflation in the memory of man' (*ibid.*, p. 458) was

---

[43] Saul (1969) reviews relevant literature concerning Great Britain. Shields (1969) offers an analysis of circumstances in the United States that accords more-or-less with my own discussion of the UK. See also some pertinent remarks by Friedman and Schwartz (1963, e.g. pp. 88, 187, and 242), who observe that US evidence for most of the period 1873-1896 'seems to run sharply counter to' the strongly held view that 'sharply declining prices [are] incompatible with sharply rising output' (*ibid.*, p. 88).

both evidence and cause of what Josiah Stamp (1931, p. 26) called 'a chronic depression in trade'.

The decades-long decline in prices has been termed 'the essential problem of the Great Depression' (Coppock, 1961, p. 205). In what sense was it a problem? Basically, because the popular linking of deflation with depression was contradicted by all sorts of other evidence. As early as 1877 Robert Giffen (1904, p. 108) found himself countering the 'common impression' that a depression of unprecedented severity was in progress. 'The common impression', Giffen insisted, 'is wrong, and the facts are entirely the other way.' Despite a drop in Britain's foreign trade and a series of poor harvests, which were serious enough, 'the community as a whole,' Giffen argued (*ibid.*, p. 109), was 'not really poorer by the pricking of all these bladders'. In support of his revisionism, Giffen presented statistics showing the lack of any 'depression'-era decline in nominal income or wages per head (*ibid.*, pp. 178-9; compare Bowley, 1920, pp. 9ff). Giffen's data actually show a distinct *upward* trend in both *per capita* taxable incomes and *per capita* nominal wages commencing with the year 1880.

Friedman and Schwartz's more recent figures (1982, Table 4.9), shown in Table 1, tell a similar story: although *per-capita* nominal income declines very gradually from 1873 to 1879, that decline was more than offset by a gradual increase over the course of the next 17 years.[44] Finally and most significantly, *real per-capita* income either stayed approximately constant (1873-1880; 1883-1885) or rose (1881-1882; 1886-1896), so that the average consumer appears to have been considerably better off at the end of the 'depression' than before. Studies of other countries where prices also tumbled, including the US, Germany, France, and Italy, reported more markedly positive trends in both nominal and real *per-capita* income figures. Profits generally were also not adversely affected by deflation, although they declined (particularly in Britain) in industries that were struggling against superior, foreign competition (Musson, 1959, p. 292). Accompanying

---

[44] Stability of *per-capita* income is *roughly* consistent with a labour productivity norm, assuming no substantial improvement in the overall skills or quality of the labour force. A total factor productivity norm would then require some growth in *per-capita* incomes corresponding to any increase in the capital intensity of production.

the overall growth in real prosperity was a marked shift in consumption from necessities to luxuries (Landes, 1965, p. 469): by 1885, according to Beales (1934, p. 74), 'more houses were being built, twice as much tea was being consumed, and even the working classes were eating imported meat, oranges, and dairy produce in quantities unprecedented'. The change in working class incomes and tastes was symbolised by 'the spectacular development of the department store and the chain store' (Landes, 1965, p. 471). In short, the Great Depression of 1873-96, considered as a depression of anything *except* the price level, appears to be a myth:

'Prices certainly fell, but almost every other index of economic activity – output of coal and pig iron, tonnage of ships built, consumption of raw wool and cotton, import and export figures, shipping entries and clearances, railway freight clearances, joint-stock company formations, trading profits, consumption per head of wheat, meat, tea, beer, and tobacco – all of these showed an upward trend.' (Musson, 1959, p. 199)

How can the myth – and its persistence – be explained? Partly it springs from the fact that certain branches of economic activity *were* indeed depressed between 1873 and 1896; in Britain these included foreign trade prior to 1875, agriculture in the late 1870s, and (as a result of increased foreign competitiveness) 'basic industries' such as the iron industry beginning in the 1880s. These troubled sectors of the economy were a source of increased structural unemployment and of 'continuous ululations of business people' (Beales, 1934, p. 66) inspiring calls for 'reciprocity' and 'fair trade' (Musson, 1959, p. 227) and provoking various royal and parliamentary inquiries. Britain and other gold standard nations were also far from being immune to genuine cyclical downturns, sometimes lasting several years and interrupting the otherwise positive trend of *per-capita* real income.

But neither sectoral troubles nor genuine cyclical downturns can account for the persistent belief that Britain suffered an 'unprecedented' depression lasting over two decades. As Landes observes (1965, p. 465), that belief has been based 'more on theoretical deductions, political dogma, and sympathy' for the truly affected groups than on any real evidence. The crucial 'theoretical deduction' in this case has consisted of the popular belief,to which some zero inflationists

TABLE 1:
Real and Nominal Income and Prices, United Kingdom, 1871-1899*

Year	Population (millions)	Nominal Income(Y) (£million)	Y/cap (£)	Real Income(y) (£million)	y/cap (£)	Price Deflator (1929=100)
1871	31·556	972	30·80	1,682	53·50	57·8
1872	31·874	1,037	32·53	1,689	52·99	61·4
1873	32·177	1,111	34·53	1,750	54·39	63·5
1874	32·501	1,084	33·35	1,763	54·24	61·5
1875	32·839	1,072	32·64	1,811	55·15	59·2
1876	33·200	1,056	31·81	1,827	55·93	57·8
1877	33·576	1,047	31·18	1,863	55·49	56·2
1878	33·932	1,015	29·91	1,839	54·20	55·2
1879	34·304	994	28·98	1,883	54·89	52·8
1880	34·623	1,037	29·95	1,885	54·44	55·0
1881	34·935	1,076	30·80	2,000	57·25	53·8
1882	35·206	1,116	31·70	2,044	58·06	54·6
1883	35·450	1,102	31·09	2,041	57·57	54·0
1884	35·724	1,073	30·04	2,044	57·21	52·4
1885	36·015	1,058	29·38	2,070	57·48	51·1
1886	36·313	1,082	29·80	2,151	59·23	50·3
1887	36·598	1,127	30·79	2,232	60·99	50·5
1888	36·881	1,204	32·65	2,384	64·64	50·5
1889	37·178	1,296	34·86	2,531	68·08	51·2
1890	37·485	1,326	35·37	2,545	67·89	52·1
1891	37·802	1,307	34·57	2,518	66·61	51·9
1892	38·134	1,268	33·25	2,448	64·19	51·8
1893	38·490	1,274	33·10	2,474	64·28	51·5
1894	38·859	1,362	35·05	2,692	69·28	50·6
1895	39·221	1,395	35·57	2,796	71·72	49·9
1896	39·599	1,431	36·14	2,879	72·70	49·7
1897	39·987	1,481	37·07	2,950	73·77	50·2
1898	40·381	1,563	38·71	3,095	76·64	50·5
1899	40·773	1,649	40·44	3,221	79·00	51·1

*Including Southern Ireland

Source: Friedman and Schwartz (1982, Table 4.9).

still subscribe, that 'falling prices curtail production...and thereby reduce wealth and well-being' (Warren and Pearson, 1933, p. 298).

Where deflation is linked to a contraction of nominal spending, or a failure of spending to keep step with growth in the labour force or capital stock, one may be justified in viewing it as a symptom, if not a cause, of depression. But a large part at least of the deflation commencing in the 1870s was a reflection of unprecedented advances in factor productivity. Real unit production costs for most final goods dropped steadily throughout the 19th century, and especially from 1873 to 1896. At no previous time, according to Landes (1965, p. 462), had there been an equivalent 'harvest of [technological] advances...so general in their application and so radical in their implications'. That is why, notwithstanding the dire predictions of many eminent economists, Britain did not end up paralysed by strikes and lock-outs. Falling prices did not mean falling money wages. Instead of inspiring large numbers of workers to go on strike, falling prices were inspiring them to go shopping!

Incidentally, Arthur Pigou (1924, pp. 70-71) once pointed out the irony that, if there ever was a protracted 'depression' at the end of the 19th century, it occurred, not during the oft-maligned era of falling prices, but immediately afterwards, when output prices began to *rise*:

> 'Whereas during the twenty years before 1896 the trend of general prices had been downwards and the rate of real wages had been rising, the reversal of the price trend in the later nineties was accompanied by a check to the upward movement of real wages. Indeed, apart from the shifting of people from lower paid to higher paid occupations, the rate of real wages actually declined between the later nineties and the outbreak of the Great War.'

The World War I Price Inflation

World War I confronted Western Europe with its most serious outbreak of inflation since the Napoleonic wars. Price-level stabilisationists came out in force, blaming the inflation entirely on excessive expansion of bank credit, and implying that a constant price level would have been more consistent with overall equilibrium.

In his own attempt to assess the wartime inflation Swedish economist David Davidson came up with an 'index of scarcity' showing the extent to which the inflation was due to real as opposed to monetary factors (Uhr, 1975, p. 297). Davidson subtracted his scarcity index from an index of wholesale prices to obtain a residual representing the truly monetary component of the inflation, that is, the component reflecting growth in aggregate nominal spending. Although his method was certainly crude (for one thing, he simply assumed a constant velocity of money), Davidson's results, shown in Table 2, are still suggestive.

As the figures show, Davidson was far from denying that Sweden's monetary policies were partly responsible for that country's wartime inflation. He did insist, however, that some of this inflation had been a reflection of increased commodity scarcity, due to reduced imports of raw materials to supplement Swedish output and to maintain its own facilities for agricultural and industrial production. To the extent that inflation resulted from the latter cause, Davidson argued, any effort to combat it by monetary restraint would have been counterproductive. In contrast, proponents of price-level stabilisation, including Davidson's compatriot Gustav Cassel, downplayed or ignored the rôle of commodity scarcity and reduced productivity in wartime price increases. Cassel blamed

TABLE 2:
Real and Monetary Causes of Inflation in Sweden, 1914-1922, according to D. Davidson

Year	Index of Wholesale Prices (1)	Index of Commodity Scarcity (2)	'Monetary' Inflation (3)=(1)-(2)	(3) as % of (1)-100
1914	100	100	0	0
1917	244	162	82	57
1918	339	151	188	79
1919	330	132	198	86
1920	340	126	221	92
1921	211	106	105	95
1922	162	101	61	98

Source: Adapted from Uhr (1975, p. 297).

the Riksbank for not restricting the money stock enough to keep prices stable. In the United States Warren and Pearson (1933, p. 116) took a similar stand, blaming high wartime US prices entirely on the Fed's failure aggressively to sterilise gold inflows, even while admitting that 'man cannot fight and produce at the same time' and that output had 'strikingly decreased' in the course of the war (*ibid.*, p. 49).

Even putting aside the question of wartime finance, it should be obvious that a policy of monetary contraction to stabilise the price level during wartime would not generally be consistent with a goal of keeping real economic variables at their natural levels. War involves a diversion, often substantial, of resources away from normal productive activities, some actual destruction of output, capital, and labour, and a general undermining of productive efficiency owing to the disruption of supply lines, communications, and the like. *Some* wartime inflation is, therefore, likely to be perfectly consistent with keeping an economy on its 'natural' path. What monetary authorities should attempt to resist is, not a rise in prices reflecting the adverse effects of war on productivity, but any *additional* rise in prices stemming from the authorities' failure to keep the money stock within bounds consistent with a more-or-less stable flow of nominal income.

The 'Relative' Inflation of the 1920s

The productivity norm also sheds light on the contribution of monetary expansion to the stock market boom and crash of the 1920s. Many present-day writers, and monetarists especially, view stability of the price level during the 1920s as a sign of general macro-economic stability and as proof that no monetary over-expansion was then in progress. These theorists all view the Great Depression as a consequence of deflationary developments commencing in the next decade.

Contemporary proponents of the productivity norm – including Dennis Robertson, Friedrich Hayek, and Harvard's John H. Williams – saw things differently. To them the 1920s represented an era of 'relative' inflation – with output prices rising *relative to unit costs*, and consequent expansion of money profits, all hidden behind a mask of stable prices.[45] In these

---

[45] Phillips, Nelson, and McManus (1937) offer a fascinating, but sadly overlooked, 'relative inflation' perspective on the 1920s boom and subsequent crash.

TABLE 3:
Real and Nominal Income and Prices: United States,
1921-1929

Year	Population (millions)	Nominal Income (Y) ($billion)	Y/cap ($)	Real Income (y) ($billion)	y/cap ($)	Price Deflator (1929=100)
1921	108·538	61·763	569	59·567	549	103·7
1922	110·049	62·996	572	63·859	580	98·6
1923	111·947	74·095	662	73·460	656	100·9
1924	114·109	75·235	659	75·559	662	99·6
1925	115·829	78·602	679	77·343	668	101·6
1926	117·397	84·566	720	82·807	705	102·1
1927	119·035	83·104	698	83·623	703	99·4
1928	120·509	84·980	705	84·918	705	100·1
1929	121·767	90·320	742	90·308	742	100·0

Source: Friedman and Schwartz (1982, Table 4.8).

economists' opinion, monetary expansion prevented a fall in prices that should have been allowed to reflect improvements in total factor productivity: although the M2 money stock grew by an average annual rate of 4·6 per cent between July 1921 and August 1929 (Friedman and Schwartz, 1963, p.274), labour productivity grew even faster (Phillips, Nelson and McManus, 1937, p. 188). The growth in productivity was therefore rapid enough to keep prices from rising despite substantial growth in both total and *per-capita* spending. Table 3 presents some relevant statistics.

Instead of being evident in rising prices, relative inflation mainly revealed itself in firms' profit statements. Business revenues and profits kept pace with money incomes generally, suggesting that nominal factor prices were relatively slow to adjust. According to a report issued by the Federal Reserve Bank of New York, profits in a sample of 99 industrial companies increased from $416 million in 1924 to $1,065 million in 1929 (Hawtrey, 1932, p. 45). Stock prices – reflecting the discounted value of anticipated future profits – rose even more dramatically, implying a general expectation that costs would not catch up with or overtake expanded earnings or that real interest rates would remain low or both. In fact, total wages rose much less rapidly than firms' revenues,

56

increasing by only about 6 per cent between 1923 and 1929 (*ibid.*, p. 47) – evidence of both sluggish adjustment of wage-rates and the tendency firms had of using profits to acquire new capital.

As long as costs lagged behind earnings, monetary expansion served to keep interest rates below their 'natural' levels, fuelling speculation. But this would cease to be the case once factor prices had risen proportionately with earnings, causing a more aggressive outward shift in the demand for loanable funds. The boom would then come to an end, unless the monetary authorities managed to sustain it by means of an accelerated rate of growth of aggregate spending. A comparison here with the Britain's earlier 'Great Depression' is instructive, for during that earlier episode most measures of aggregate spending were more-or-less constant.

Proponents of the productivity norm viewed the stock market crash as an inevitable consequence of relative inflation that preceded it.[46] Writing just before the crash, Robertson (1928, p. 68) complained that 'in so far as the Federal System has not gone all out for stabilising the price of *labour*, it cannot, I think, be wholly absolved from the charge of having burgled the public in these years of rapidly advancing productivity' by holding interest rates below their 'natural' levels. Robertson was referring to the link connecting 'easy money' with 'forced saving', an important cause, in his view, of unsustainable business-cycle upswings. After the crash, Robertson (1931, p. 45) looked back upon policies of the preceding years as

'a vast attempt to destabilise the value of money in terms of human effort by means of a colossal programme of investment...which succeeded for a surprisingly long period, but which no human ingenuity could have managed to direct indefinitely on sound and balanced lines'.

The Federal Reserve itself took a similar stance: in its *Bulletin* (1937, pp. 827-28), the Board admitted that 'unstable conditions may develop, as they did in the 1920s, while the price level remains stable', and declared that a falling price

---

[46] Chandler (1971, p. 20), in contrast, admits that 'a case can indeed be made for a declining price level reflecting increasing productivity per unit of inputs', but says that 'it is by no means clear that a stable price level under these conditions' is injurious.

level would have made a greater contribution 'toward the maintenance of [overall] stability'.

In reply to the claim that price-level stabilisation had fuelled the stock-market boom and subsequent collapse, some proponents of price-level stability argue that it failed only in the sense that it was not continued after 1929 (for example, Bach, 1940, p. 122; Mints, 1950, p. 131). But while absolute deflation undoubtedly contributed to the depression after 1930, it cannot be blamed for the 1929 stock market crash: during the 12 months leading to the collapse in stock prices, both wholesale prices and the implicit price index were practically flat, and so was the velocity of money. Income continued to rise, although less rapidly than in preceding months, thanks to a still-expanding money stock (Friedman and Schwartz, 1963, chart 62). The Fed was certainly guilty of letting the boom end when it might have tried to prolong it, and of allowing a subsequent outbreak of deflation. But it does not follow that high stock prices could have been maintained without resort to outright inflation: in the face of rising costs, the only way to sustain positive profit expectations was by accelerating the rate of inflation, in this case from zero to something higher. Productivity-norm theorists viewed the stock market crash as the starting point of a malinvestment liquidation process as well as of the downward slide in confidence (which monetarists emphasise) that would eventually trigger a massive monetary contraction. According to the productivity-norm view, price-level stabilisation did set the stage for the depression, by fuelling an unsustainable expansion of stock prices that a productivity norm might have avoided.

It should be stressed that, in endorsing the 'relative inflation' view, the intention is not to downplay the rôle of *deflation*, both relative and absolute, in deepening and prolonging the depression of the 1930s – a genuine rather than mythical 'Great Depression'. Indeed, the relative inflation of the previous decade is only likely to have played a relatively minor part in explaining the length and severity of the depression, in contrast to its major rôle in causing the stock-market boom and crash. Some early proponents of a productivity norm – the 'Austrian' economists especially – failed to acknowledge this fact, or acknowledged it only belatedly, suggesting that the depression in all its severity was solely a 'correction' of previous maladjustments, and arguing against any resort to expansionary monetary policies, even when they would merely have served to stabilise nominal spending and income.[47] Such advice was inconsistent with a genuine productivity norm, which calls for monetary expansion to prevent any deflation not consistent with improvements in factor productivity. Sadly, in failing to take a vigorous stand against the deflationary policies of the early 1930s, economists of the Austrian school unwittingly encouraged later generations of theorists to dismiss wholly valid arguments favouring deflation in non-crisis times.

The 1973-74 Oil and Agricultural Supply Shocks[48]

The importance of appropriate price-level policy was brought home more recently by the oil and agricultural crises of the early 1970s. These crises had an enduring adverse effect on overall productivity (Tatom, 1979). While the crises were unfolding, monetarists, including Allan Meltzer (1974), Milton Friedman (1974), and Robert Barro (1976), argued for more aggressive contraction of money and credit to counteract accelerating inflation, without bothering to distinguish between price movements linked to expanded spending and movements consistent with reduced productivity.[49] Others, including Alan Blinder (1981), Edmund Phelps (1978), Robert Gordon (1975), and Arthur Okun (1980, pp. 253-55) argued for greater monetary

---

[47] On Hayek's views in particular see Haberler (1986) and Selgin (1995b).

[48] Recent writers, for example Taylor (1985), have adopted the misleading practice of referring to (negative) supply shocks as 'price shocks', as if an increase in aggregate spending could not also cause the price level to rise unexpectedly.

[49] This prescription was not based upon ignorance as to what was happening to real costs. On the contrary: some argued explicitly that increased real costs do not justify departure from a constant price-level rule. Thus Barro (1976, p. 3) wrote that '[a]dverse shifts like the oil and agricultural crises will reduce output and cause painful relative adjustments no matter what the reaction of the monetary authority. Added monetary noise would only complicate and lengthen the process of adjustment'. Note how Barro treats any change in the price level as a source of 'monetary noise', whether or not the change reflects a change in total spending. Robert Hall (1984, p. 308) took a similar stand in observing that 'the corrective action' by the monetary authorities 'must be more than a nudge' whenever 'a sharp movement in the price level comes from oil, agriculture, or elsewhere'.

expansion – which would have meant *more* inflation – to 'accommodate' the adverse supply shocks and dampen their labour-market effects. Both sides in this controversy overlooked a third policy option – the productivity norm – according to which the money stock should have remained more-or-less constant (depending, as explained below, on the elasticity of demand for money balances), allowing prices to increase in proportion to the rise in unit real costs of production, but no further, and allowing the supply of labour to decline only to the extent that the decline was warranted by lowered real wages.

Of course, a 'passive' monetary policy – one that neither reduces nor expands the stock of money – is not always appropriate following a supply (productivity) shock. Whether it is depends on the (real) income elasticity of the demand for money. A passive policy is called for if the demand for money is 'unit elastic' – meaning that the real value of the public's desired holdings of money is strictly proportional to the public's real earnings, *ceteris paribus*. If the demand for money is elastic or inelastic relative to real income, even a productivity norm requires some adjustment of the money stock following a productivity change. If the demand for money is elastic relative to real income, so that an increase in real income leads to a more than proportionate increase in the demand for real money balances, an increase in productivity requires an increase in the money stock to ensure that prices fall in proportion with the increase in productivity but no further. If the demand for money is inelastic relative to real income, an increase in productivity requires some reduction in the money stock to make prices fall sufficiently.

To the extent that pleas for 'accommodating' supply shocks were grounded in evidence of an inelastic demand for money, accommodation would have been entirely consistent with a productivity norm. But, as Stanley Fischer (1985, pp. 1-2) has observed, an accommodative response to supply shocks is not *generally* warranted:

> '[S]upply shocks by themselves are unlikely to lead to unemployment if monetary policy remains passive and so long as there is no real wage resistance by workers. It is rather the aggregate demand effects associated with supply shocks – including counter-inflationary policy responses – that are responsible for unemployment.'

When the demand for money is unit-elastic relative to real income, prices will automatically rise in proportion with fallen output, and real wages will fall correspondingly (*ibid.*, p. 8).

It is far from clear, moreover, that the demand for money was in fact inelastic when the oil crisis struck. According to Milton Friedman and Anna Schwartz (1982, p. 233), money's real-income elasticity has had a value of about 1·2 over the last century or so, allowing for a post-war shift in the demand for money. According to this estimate, money is more a 'luxury' than a necessity – meaning that, if anything, its stock ought to be reduced in response to any setback to productivity.

That the money stock (and aggregate spending) actually grew too fast during the oil crisis seems evident from data, summarised in Table 4, showing rapid growth in both total and *per-capita* spending. These figures offer further evidence that the demand for money relative to real income did not increase. A result of this was that, as in the case of the First World War inflation in Sweden and elsewhere, the price level rose more than in inverse proportion to the fall in productivity and real output *per capita*. The monetarists were therefore justified in claiming that the money stock was growing too rapidly. They went too far, though, in suggesting that the most appropriate rate of expansion was one that would have kept the price level from rising at all.[50]

A distinct argument for 'accommodating' supply shocks, which often appears alongside the previously discussed argument, does not require an inelastic demand for money. It assumes instead that the *goods* (such as fuel-oil and produce) whose output is most directly affected by supply shocks are ones for which demand is relatively inelastic. An adverse supply shock will then cause spending on these goods to increase. This means that, even if aggregate spending remains

---

[50] A referee suggests that I may be being unfair to the monetarists: after all, he observes, most monetarists would rather not let central bankers have the discretion that might be needed to allow them to minimise the harmful consequences of each and every shock to which the economy may be exposed. According to this view, an occasional, less than ideal policy response is a price worth paying so that central bankers will not have a licence to abuse their power. I sympathise with this view. Nevertheless, the fact is that there was no price-level stability rule in effect when the oil-shock struck. Given this context, it seems to me that monetarists who argued for monetary tightening sufficient to stabilise the price level were arguing for something beyond mere adherence to a monetary rule.

TABLE 4:
Real and Nominal Income and Prices: United States, 1970-1975

Year	Population (millions)	Nominal Income (Y) ($billion)	Y/cap ($)	Real Income (y) ($billion)	y/cap ($)	Price Deflator (1929=100)
1970	204·878	740·587	3,615	296·591	1,448	249·7
1971	207·053	801·277	3,870	304·546	1,471	263·2
1972	208·846	885·254	4,239	316·389	1,515	279·8
1973	210·410	987·543	4,693	330·352	1,570	298·9
1974	211·901	1,059·479	5,000	330·621	1,560	321·7
1975	213·540	1,125·473	5,271	324·812	1,521	346·5

Source: Friedman and Schwartz (1982, Table 4.8).

stable, the demand for other products, and their producers' revenues, must fall. If money wages are rigid, workers in *non*-supply-shocked industries may end up unemployed unless the monetary authorities take steps, not merely to sustain, but to *expand*, aggregate spending.[51]

But this argument proves too much. For if an expansion of the money stock is warranted to prevent, not a general decline in spending, but a decline affecting certain industries only and matched by an equal expansion of spending elsewhere, then monetary expansion would seem to be justified, not just in response to an adverse supply shock, but also in connection with *any* shift in demand from one set of producers to another. For here no less than in the supply-shock case *some* producers are affected 'just as they would be by a one-time reduction in [aggregate spending].' (Okun, 1980, p. 254)

---

[51] A peculiar asymmetry seems to affect arguments for monetary 'accommodation'. One never encounters the opinion that a *positive* productivity or supply shock directly affecting goods in inelastic demand should be 'accommodated' through a forced *reduction* in aggregate spending. Richard Lipsey (1990, p. 28) illustrates this asymmetry quite clearly in observing that, because economies are 'subject to periodic supply-side shocks', it may be desirable to prefer 'a target of some modest, positive rate [of inflation] – say, 2 per cent – rather than zero'. The argument seems to assume that all supply shocks are negative ones, as if positive 'shocks' were not (by definition) just as frequent.

Consistently applied, the above reasoning amounts to a recipe for high inflation: the money stock would have to be expanded sufficiently rapidly to maintain a fixed level of revenue even in industries whose output is no longer wanted by anyone! Moreover the reasoning simply overlooks the fact that it is perfectly desirable to allow spending on certain goods to decline in response to a *relative* decline in the demand for those goods, even if that means letting certain industries become 'depressed'.

Years before OPEC, zero-inflationist Lloyd Mints (1950, pp. 117-18) seemed to anticipate accommodationists' reasoning in pointing out that 'Monetary action is not appropriate as a remedial measure for the economic ills of specific areas, industries, or groups of consumers or producers'. We must, after all, insist on a distinction between shocks that depress the *overall* value of money wages (which the monetary authorities ought to combat), and ones that merely alter the *relative distribution* of money wages (which the authorities ought to ignore).

Is offering the above monetary policy prescription brushing aside sectoral unemployment problems resulting from rigid money wage-rates? There will, indeed, be some increase in frictional and structural unemployment following the sort of industry-specific shocks discussed above. But the presence of rigid money wage-rates (which might seem to justify turning-on the money spigot to stop the unemployment) turns out to be something of a red herring, since (as we saw earlier) the situations being contemplated are ones where, given that labour mobility equalises wage-rates across industries, *even relative money wage-rates do not necessarily have to change.* In fact, as Fritz Machlup (1952, pp. 403-04) once noted, any supply-shock-induced difference between nominal wages in relatively depressed industries and those in relatively prosperous ones is inconsistent with a competitive general equilibrium if it means having certain industries 'pay higher wages for the same kind of work that rates lower wages elsewhere'.

V. THE PRODUCTIVITY NORM IN PRACTICE

The Productivity Norm and Nominal Income Targeting

Were a productivity norm put into practice, a stable price level would be observed only under conditions of constant factor productivity. As productivity grew, prices would fall. If past estimates of aggregate productivity growth rates are any guide, a secular decline in prices of between one and three per cent per year (depending on how productivity is measured) could be expected in 'normal' times. Exceptions would be periods of extraordinary progress, when prices would fall more rapidly than usual, and periods of increased scarcity and reduced output *per capita*, such as during wars, harvest failures, and other 'supply shocks', when prices would rise, perhaps sharply.

Just how does one put a productivity norm into practice? Although a number of alternative procedures might be considered, perhaps the most practical of them would be a version of nominal income (GNP or GDP) targeting, the general advantages of which have been set forth by Bennett McCallum and others.[52] Because these writers view nominal income targeting as a means of achieving long-run price-level stability, they would have the central bank aim for a growth rate of nominal income equal to the (natural) growth rate of real output. They would, in other words, allow innovations to productivity to have only temporary price-level effects. But nominal income can just as easily be targeted in a manner consistent with a productivity norm, by having the monetary authorities aim for a growth rate of nominal income equal to the growth rate of real factor (labour or labour and capital) input. This moving income target would allow permanent changes in the price level reflecting permanent changes (including anticipated changes) in productivity.

Which Productivity Norm?

Until now the implications of 'a productivity norm' have been considered without bothering to distinguish between *labour* productivity and *total factor* productivity. As noted previously,

---

[52] See the references in note 30 (above, p. 34).

the distinction is irrelevant in a world where the ratio of capital to labour input is not changing. In the real, industrialised world, however, the capital-labour ratio does change, mainly by growing over time.

Because improvements in labour productivity reflect both improvements in total factor productivity and more capital-intensive production, a labour productivity norm would tend to be more deflationary than a total factor productivity norm: implementing such a norm means setting the growth rate of nominal income equal to the expected growth rate of (quality-adjusted) labour input.[53] As the capital-labour ratio changes, holding the quality and composition of the labour stock constant, money wage-rates remain unchanged, and real wage-rates are kept in line with an improving marginal product of labour entirely by means of falling output prices. The rental price of capital must, in contrast, decline in proportion to the decline in capital's marginal product as production becomes more capital intensive. To the extent that labour input is less subject to measurement errors than the input of capital services, a labour productivity norm might be put into effect with greater accuracy than its total-factor productivity counterpart. Finally, because it is more deflationary, a labour productivity norm would come closer than would a total factor productivity norm to achieving an 'optimum' money stock.

A total factor productivity norm involves setting the growth rate of nominal income equal to an average of expected labour and capital input growth rates, where the growth rate of each factor is weighted by its share of producers' expenses. Such a norm would therefore stabilise, not money wage-rates, but an index of factor prices, so that money wages increase somewhat as production becomes more capital-intensive and decline on those more rare occasions in which production becomes less capital intensive. The rental price of capital goods would, consequently, not have to adjust as much in response to any given change in capital's marginal product as it would under a labour productivity norm. Moreover, price-level movements would be more closely related to changes in real unit production costs. Finally, although the amount of real capital input is more subject to measurement error than

---

[53] See the Appendix (below, pp.72-3) for a formal demonstration of this and other statements made in this section.

the amount of labour input, popular measurements all suggest a relatively stable growth rate of capital input. This means that a total factor productivity norm will be less subject to input forecast (as opposed to measurement) errors than a labour productivity norm.

So which option is more consistent with overall macro-economic stability? The answer is far from obvious, and the question warrants further research. For the moment, I am inclined to favour the total factor productivity option on pragmatic grounds: as long as the capital-labour ratio does not change, a total factor productivity norm is equivalent to a labour productivity norm; when the capital-labour ratio *does* change but total factor productivity does not, a total factor productivity norm is equivalent to zero inflation. A total factor productivity norm therefore represents something of a compromise between a labour productivity norm and a zero inflation norm, making it the less controversial and *politically* more attractive option, as well as a useful stepping-stone from zero inflation to a 'labour standard', should the latter ultimately prove better in theory.

It is also relevant to observe that, regardless of its precise form, a real-world productivity norm is bound to be far from perfect. This has to be so, not only because we often face a choice between keeping wages stable on one hand and keeping prices in line with real unit costs on the other, but also because of the great difficulties involved in measuring and forecasting the growth rates of labour and capital input. To be sure, measurements of real output growth are themselves fraught with problems (Morgenstern, 1963, Chap. 14); while the extreme volatility of productivity itself makes forecasting real output growth far more difficult (measurement errors aside) than forecasting real input growth.[54] The real choice we face is, therefore, not really a choice between a true productivity norm or a truly constant price level, but between some crude approximation of a productivity norm and some equally crude approximation of a constant price level.

---

[54] In the United States between 1948 and 1981, the annualised peak-to-peak growth rate of real output varied from 6·59 per cent to *minus* 0·0024 per cent – a standard deviation of 2·697 (Bureau of Labor Statistics, 1983). This mainly reflects the underlying volatility of productivity growth. The standard deviation of the peak-to-peak growth rate of labour input during the same period was only 1·03; the standard deviation of the capital input growth rate was still smaller.

A Free-Banking Alternative

Monetary authorities attempting to target spending can also err by misforecasting changes in the velocity of money and the high-powered or base-money multiplier. Such errors can, however, be avoided by reforming national monetary arrangements. The reform I have in mind would make it much easier to achieve any chosen nominal income target, while also substantially lowering the need for central-bank discretion. Best of all, the needed reform is, largely, one that is already taking place around the globe, albeit slowly and unevenly. I refer to the deregulation of banks and other private monetary institutions, and especially the removal of statutory reserve requirements and restrictions on private firms' ability to issue substitutes (paper, plastic or electronic) for government-issued paper currency.

How could a comprehensively deregulated or 'free' banking system assist the implementation of a productivity norm? Free banking could help by making for a relatively stable relationship between the volume of aggregate spending (the one thing the central bank *needs* to control) and the quantity of central-bank-created base money (the one thing it definitely *can* control). To see how, imagine a banking system in which private substitutes have completely displaced government currency holdings in the hands of the public,[55] and which is free from all statutory reserve requirements. Banks in this system still need to keep reserves of government base money to settle daily interbank debts. So what determines the overall demand for bank reserves? The answer, according to received theory, is that the demand for reserves will be a function, like that shown in Figure 5, of the total volume of (gross) interbank transactions, where that volume itself is proportional to nominal income. It follows that any *given* quantity of base money reserves will support a definite level of nominal income – the level that generates a demand for reserves equal to the available supply – no more, no less.[56]

---

[55] It makes no difference if some quantity of government currency remains in circulation, so long as that quantity stays relatively constant, instead of being deposited in banks.

[56] See Selgin (1994). More general treatments of free banking include Dowd (1988, 1989), Selgin (1988, 1996a), Selgin and White (1994), and White (1989). Milton Friedman (1984, pp. 49-50) was the first economist to suggest a monetary reform combining free banking with a frozen stock of fiat base money. See note 58 below.

Figure 5: Reserve and Nominal Income Equilibria under Free Banking with a Fixed Stock of Reserves

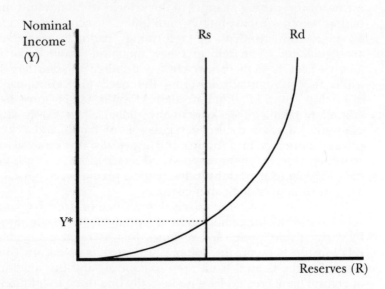

Next, consider the implications of a change in the velocity of money, starting from a situation of supply-demand equilibrium in the market for bank reserves. Suppose velocity falls. Then nominal income also falls, giving rise to an excess supply of bank reserves. Given a fixed stock of reserves, individual banks try to lend out their share of the excess which, in hot-potato fashion, merely gets tossed around a bit by the banks without ever actually leaving the banking system. The tossing-around process is, however, one that expands the quantity of bank money until the old level of aggregate spending is restored. The excess supply of reserves thus gets eliminated, since the demand for reserves rises again, in effect 'cooling' the hot potato. An increase in velocity has similar consequences, except that the money stock shrinks instead of expanding.

In short, a free-banking system, given some fixed quantity of base money to work with, *tends automatically to stabilise nominal income.*[57] Getting nominal income to grow at some

---

[57] The qualifier 'tends' is important: changes in interest rates may alter the relationship between nominal income and the quantity of base money, by

predetermined rate then becomes a relatively simple matter of having the central bank expand the stock of base money by that rate.[58] As monetarists will be especially quick to see, enforcing this kind of central bank rule does not take a Board of Governors, a Chancellor of the Exchequer, or a caucus of economists. A computer will do, provided it is fed the necessary information regarding changes (or predicted changes) in factor supply. This adds to the beauty of the reform, because a computer, unlike a person or committee, will not change its mind, or go back on its word.

---

changing banks' desired reserve ratios. Fortunately, studies suggest that the demand for prudential bank reserves is interest-inelastic. Of greater concern are changes in payments habits and technology, which may have more substantial consequences. With luck, such changes will occur only gradually, and will therefore not prove overly disruptive. The changes are, in any event, likely to be ones leading to a reduced demand for base money and consequent higher ratio of nominal income per base dollar. This risk of occasional (relative) inflation has to be weighed against the well-established inflationary tendencies of central banks. Institutions, like people, are never perfect.

[58] This argument does not take into account financial innovations that might reduce banks' demand for reserves independently of any change in the velocity of money. Some time ago, Milton Friedman (1984, pp. 48-50) argued for deregulating banks while *freezing* the stock of base money. Although Friedman recognised that this policy might lead, in the absence of financial innovations, to deflation at a rate equal to the growth rate of real output (hence exceeding the growth rate of productivity), he believed that financial innovations would work in practice to counter much of the deflation.

VI. CONCLUSION

Zero inflationists offer a largely sound and sober view of what monetary policy can and cannot accomplish. They understand that secular inflation contributes nothing to economic progress, and that policy should seek to do no more than keep real output and employment at 'natural' levels consistent with an efficient overall use of resources.

But zero inflationists have been advocating a monetary policy target that at best only crudely achieves their ultimate policy goals. In the face of innovations to aggregate productivity, a constant price level cannot be relied upon to avoid 'unnatural' fluctuations in output and employment. A productivity norm, involving secular deflation interrupted by occasional negative supply shocks, would be far better able to achieve the zero inflationists' own ultimate objectives. In particular, compared to zero inflation, a productivity norm:

(1) is likely to involve lower 'menu' costs of price adjustment;
(2) is less likely to invite monetary misperception effects;
(3) is more conducive to the achievement of efficient outcomes using fixed money contracts; and
(4) generally keeps the money stock closer to its 'optimum' level.

Yet the productivity norm idea continues to languish, while zero inflation grows ever more popular. Faulty analysis is, as suggested above, one explanation for this. But there is another. This is that zero inflationists have been busy wrestling with arguments for secular inflation. Not long ago they confronted a world economy hooked on double-digit inflation, where any proposal for reducing inflation was regarded as a recipe for depression, and where proposals for zero inflation were considered both cruel and utopian. We should not wonder that, under such circumstances, few persons bothered to think about, let alone argue for, secularly falling prices.[59] And who could blame them? It was, after all, a case of not letting the best be the enemy of the good.

---

[59] Milton Friedman did, of course, offer his 'Optimum Quantity of Money' argument for deflation in 1969; but until relatively recently Friedman, in his

Fortunately the zero inflationists have prevailed, and world inflation rates have fallen. In several countries, allowing for some positive bias in popular inflation measures, zero inflation itself is now close to being the *status quo*. That is a great accomplishment in its own right. But its full benefits will not be grasped unless we recognise it as a stepping-stone towards something even better.

actual proposals for monetary policy, favoured rules aimed at achieving zero long-run inflation. In Friedman's case, to be sure, something more than mere pragmatism must have been behind the preference. More representative of a pragmatic approach is Arthur Okun, who asserted (1980, p. 284) that 'No government capable of influencing aggregate demand will live with a negative trend of prices. Such a trend could and did emerge a century ago when policymakers did not have the knowledge or the tools to correct it. But it could not happen today.'

APPENDIX

Productivity Norms and Nominal Income Targets

Let

$$Py = wL + rK \qquad (1)$$

represent an economy's nominal income, where P is the general price level, y is real output, w is the price of a unit of average-quality labour, r is the rental price of average-quality capital, L is labour input, and K is capital input. Also, let

$$y = AK^b L^{1-b} \qquad (2)$$

be the economy's production function, where A is a total factor productivity index and b is capital's share of total income, rK/Py, which is assumed to be constant (as is roughly the case in reality). The logarithmic differential of (2) with respect to time is:

$$y = A + bK + (1\text{-}b)L, \qquad (3)$$

where italics represent growth rates. A, then, is the growth rate of total factor productivity. Rearranging (3) gives

$$y - L = A + b(K - L) \qquad (4)$$

where $y - L$ is the growth rate of labour productivity and $K - L$ is the growth rate of the capital-labour ratio.

A labour productivity norm requires that

$$P = L - y \qquad (5)$$

whereas a total factor productivity norm requires that $P = -A$ or, equivalently (from equation 4) that

$$P = -y + bK + (1 - b)L. \qquad (6)$$

Equations (5) and (6) can be rearranged to give corresponding rules for nominal income growth. A *labour productivity norm* requires that

$$P + y = L, \qquad (7)$$

that is, that nominal income grow at the same rate as labour input; while a total factor productivity norm requires that

$$P + y = bK + (1 - b)L, \qquad (8)$$

that is, that nominal income grow at a rate equal to a weighted average of the growth rates of labour and capital input.

Lastly, we can compare the behaviour of (constant-quality) money wages under the two régimes by taking the logarithmic differential of (1) and recalling that $b = rK/Py = a$ constant:

$$P + y = w + L. \qquad (9)$$

By substituting (7) and (8), respectively, into (9), and solving in each case for w, we find that, under a labour productivity norm,

$$w = 0$$

meaning that money wages are kept stable; whereas, under a total factor productivity norm,

$$w = b(K - L),$$

meaning that money wages rise as production becomes more capital intense.

REFERENCES/FURTHER READING

Akerlof, George A., William T. Dickens, and George L. Perry (1996): 'The Macroeconomics of Low Inflation', *Brookings Papers on Economic Activity*, Vol. 1, pp.1-59.

Anonymous (1992): 'The End of Inflation?' *The Economist*, No. 322 (22 February), pp.11-12.

Arrow, Kenneth (1969): 'Toward a Theory of Price Adjustment', in M. Abramovitz, (ed.), *The Allocation of Economic Resources*, Stanford, CA: Stanford University Press, pp. 41-51.

Bailey, Samuel (1837): *Money and Its Vicissitudes in Value*, London: Effingham Wilson.

Bach, George Leland (1940): 'Price Level Stabilisation: Some Theoretical and Practical Considerations', Dissertation, University of Chicago.

Ball, Laurence, and N. Gregory Mankiw (1994): 'A Sticky-Price Manifesto', NBER Working Paper No. 4677 (March).

Barro, Robert J. (1976): 'Rational Expectations and the Rôle of Monetary Policy', *Journal of Monetary Economics*, Vol. 2 (January), pp.1-32.

Beales, H. L. (1934): '"The Great Depression" in Industry and Trade', *Economic History Review*, Vol. 5 (October), pp.65-75.

Bean, C. (1983): 'Targeting Nominal Income: An Appraisal', *Economic Journal*, Vol. 93 (December), pp.806-19.

Blinder, Alan S. (1981): 'Monetary Accommodation of Supply Shocks under Rational Expectations', *Journal of Money, Credit, and Banking*, Vol. 13 (November), pp.925-38.

Board of Governors of the Federal Reserve System (1937): *Federal Reserve Bulletin*, No. 33.

Bowley, Arthur L. (1920): *The Change in the Distribution of the National Income, 1880-1913*, Oxford: The Clarendon Press.

Bradley, Michael D., and Dennis W. Jansen (1989): 'Understanding Nominal GNP Targeting', Federal Reserve

Bank of St. Louis *Review*, No. 70 (November/December), pp.31-40.

Buchanan, James (1962): 'Predictability: The Criterion of Monetary Constitutions', in Leland B. Yeager, (ed.), *In Search of a Monetary Constitution*, Cambridge, Mass.: Harvard University Press, pp. 155-83.

Bureau of Labour Statistics (1983): *Trends in Multifactor Productivity, 1948-81*, Washington, DC.

Carlstrom, Charles T., and William T. Gavin (1993): 'Zero Inflation: Transition Costs and Shoe Leather Benefits', *Contemporary Policy Issues*, Vol. 11 (January), pp.9-17.

Chandler, Lester (1971): *American Monetary Policy, 1928-1941*, New York: Harper & Row.

Coppock, D. J. (1961): 'The Causes of the Great Depression, 1873-96', *The Manchester School*, Vol. 29 (September), pp.205-32.

Cozier, Barry, and Jack Selody (1992): 'Inflation and Macroeconomic Performance: Some Cross-Country Evidence', Ottowa: Bank of Canada Dept. of Monetary and Financial Analysis.

Dowd, Kevin (1988): *Private Money: The Path to Monetary Stability*, Hobart Paper 112, London: Institute of Economic Affairs.

_____ (1989): *The State and the Monetary System*, New York: St. Martin's Press.

_____ (1995): 'Deflating the Productivity Norm', *Journal of Macroeconomics*, Vol. 17 (Fall), pp.717-32.

Edgeworth, F.Y. (1925): *Papers Relating to Political Economy*, London: The Royal Economic Society.

Fischer, Stanley (1985): 'Supply Shocks, Wage Stickiness, and Accommodation', *Journal of Money, Credit, and Banking*, Vol. 17 (February), pp.1-15.

Fisher, Irving (1930): *The Theory of Interest*, New York: Macmillan.

_____ (1934): *Stable Money: A History of the Movement*, London: Adelphi Press.

Frankel, Jeffrey, with Menzie Chinn (1995): 'The Stabilizing Properties of a Nominal GNP Rule', *Journal of Money, Credit, and Banking*, Vol. 27 (May), pp.318-34.

Friedman, Milton (1969): 'The Optimum Quantity of Money', in idem., *The Optimum Quantity of Money and Other Essays*, Chicago: Aldine, pp. 1-50.

_____ (1974): 'Is Money Too Tight?' *Newsweek*, No. 84 (September), p. 82.

_____ (1984): 'Monetary Policy for the 1980s', in John H. Moore, (ed.), *To Promote Prosperity: U.S. Domestic Policy in the Mid-1980s*, Stanford: The Hoover Institution, pp. 48-52.

Friedman, Milton, and Anna J. Schwartz (1963): *A Monetary History of the United States, 1867-1960*, Princeton: Princeton University Press and NBER.

_____ (1982): *Monetary Trends in the United States and the United Kingdom: Their Relation to Income, Prices, and Interest Rates, 1867-1975*, Chicago: University of Chicago Press.

Gavin, William T. (1990): 'In Defense of Zero Inflation', in Robert C. York, (ed.), *Taking Aim: The Debate on Zero Inflation*, Toronto: C. D. Howe Institute, pp. 43-62.

Giffen, Sir Robert (1904): *Economic Inquiries and Studies*, Vol. 2, London: George Bell and Sons.

Gilbert, J. C. (1955): 'Changes in Productivity and the Price Level in a Closed Economy', *Yorkshire Bulletin of Economic and Social Research*, No. 8, pp.61-79.

_____ (1957): 'The Compatibility of Any Behavior of the Price Level with Equilibrium', *Review of Economic Studies*, Vol. 24 (June), pp.177-184.

Gordon, Robert J. (1975): 'Alternative Responses of Policy to External Supply Shocks', *Brookings Papers on Economic Activity*, Vol. 1, pp.183-206.

Greenfield, Robert L., and Leland Yeager (1983): 'A Laissez Faire Approach to Monetary Stability', *Journal of Money, Credit, and Banking*, Vol. 15 (August), pp.103-15.

Haberler, Gottfried (1931): 'The Different Meanings Attached to the Term Fluctuations in the Purchasing Power of Gold and the Best Instrument or Instruments for Measuring such Fluctuation', Geneva: League of Nations.

_____ (1986): 'Reflections on Hayek's Business Cycle Theory', *Cato Journal*, Vol. 6 (Fall), pp.421-35.

Hall, Robert E. (1984): 'A Free-Market Policy to Stabilize the Purchasing Power of the Dollar', in Barry N. Siegel, (ed.), *Money in Crisis.* San Francisco: Pacific Institute, pp. 303-322.

Haraf, William S. (1986): 'Monetary Velocity and Monetary Rules', *Cato Journal*, Vol. 6 (Fall), pp.641-42.

Hawtrey, Ralph G. (1930): 'Money and Index Numbers', *Journal of the Royal Statistical Society*, Vol. 93, pp.64-85.

_____. (1932): 'Speculation and Collapse in Wall Street', in *The Art of Central Banking*, London: Longmans, Green and Co.

Hayek, F. A. (1975): *'Full Employment at Any Price?'*, Institute of Economic Affairs, Occasional Paper 45.

Hetzel, Robert (1995): 'Why the Price Level Wanders Aimlessly', *Journal of Economics and Business*, Vol. 47 (May), pp.151-63.

Hoskins, W. Lee (1990): 'A U. S. Perspective on Zero Inflation', in Robert C. York, (ed.), *Taking Aim: The Debate on Zero Inflation*, Toronto: C. D. Howe Institute, pp. 34-42.

Howitt, Peter (1990): Comment on William Scarth, 'Fighting Inflation: Are the Costs of Getting to Zero Too High?', in Robert C. York (ed.), *Taking Aim: The Debate on Zero Inflation*, Toronto: C. D. Howe Institute, pp. 104-8.

Jarrett, J. P., and J. G. Selody (1982): 'The Productivity-Inflation Nexus in Canada, 1963-1979', *Review of Economics and Statistics*, Vol. 64, pp. 361-67.

Jenkins, W. Paul (1990): 'The Goal of Price Stability', in Robert C. York, (ed.), *Taking Aim: The Debate on Zero Inflation*, Toronto: C. D. Howe Institute, pp. 19-24.

Kendrick, John W., and Elliot S. Grossman (1980): *Productivity in the United States: Trends and Cycles*, Baltimore: Johns Hopkins University Press.

Keynes, John Maynard (1936): *The General Theory of Employment, Interest, and Money*, London: Macmillan.

Landes, David S. (1965): 'Technological Change and Development in Western Europe, 1750-1914', in the *Cambridge Economic History of Europe*, Vol. 6. Cambridge, UK: Cambridge University Press, pp. 274-601.

Lastrapes, William D., and George Selgin (1995): 'The Liquidity Effect: Identifying Short-Run Interest Rate Dynamics Using Long-Run Restrictions', *Journal of Macroeconomics*, Vol. 17 (Summer), pp.387-404.

Leijonhufvud, Axel (1981): *Information and Coordination*, New York: Oxford University Press.

Levitan, Sar A., and Diane Werneke (1984): *Productivity: Problems, Prospects, and Policies*, Baltimore: Johns Hopkins University Press.

Lipsey, Richard G. (1990): 'The Low Inflation Consensus', in Robert C. York, (ed.), *Taking Aim: The Debate on Zero Inflation*, Toronto: C. D. Howe Institute, pp. 25-33.

Lucas, Robert F. (1990): 'The Case for Stable, But Not Zero, Inflation', in Robert C. York, (ed.), *Taking Aim: The Debate on Zero Inflation*, Toronto: C. D. Howe Institute, pp. 65-80.

Machlup, Fritz (1952): *The Political Economy of Monopoly*, Baltimore: Johns Hopkins University Press.

McCallum, Bennett T. (1987): 'The Case for Rules in the Conduct of Monetary Policy: A Concrete Example', Federal Reserve Bank of Richmond *Economic Review*, Vol. 73 (October), pp.10-18.

_____. (1995): 'Choice of Target for Monetary Policy', *Economic Affairs*, Vol. 15 (Autumn), pp.35-41.

Meltzer, Allan H. (1974): 'A Plan for Subduing Inflation', *Fortune*, Vol. 90 (September), pp. 112-15, 210, 212.

Mints, Lloyd W. (1950): *Monetary Policy for a Competitive Society*, New York: McGraw Hill.

Morgenstern, Oscar (1963): *On the Accuracy of Economic Observations*, Princeton: Princeton University Press.

Musson, A. E. (1959): 'The Great Depression in Britain, 1873-1896', *Journal of Economic History*, Vol. 19 (June), pp.199-228.

Norsworthy, J. R. (1984): 'Growth Accounting and Productivity Measurement', *Review of Income and Wealth*, Vol. 30, pp.309-29.

Okun, Arthur (1980): *Prices and Quantities: A Macroeconomic Analysis*, Washington: Brookings Institution.

Phelps, Edmund S. (1978): 'Commodity-Supply Shocks and Full-Employment Monetary Policy', *Journal of Money, Credit, and Banking*, Vol. 10 (May), pp.206-21.

Phillips, C. A., T. F. McManus, and R. W. Nelson (1937): *Banking and the Business Cycle: A Study of the Great Depression in the United States*, New York: Macmillan.

Pigou, Arthur Cecil (1924): 'Prices and Wages from 1896-1914', in idem, *Essays in Applied Economics*, London: P. S. King & Sons, pp. 71-79.

Robertson, Dennis H. (1922): *Money*, Cambridge: Cambridge University Press.

_____. (1928): *Money*, 3rd. ed., revised, Cambridge: Cambridge University Press.

_____. (1931): 'How Do We Want Gold to Behave?' in *The International Gold Problem.*, London: Oxford University Press, pp. 18-46.

_____. (1963): 'A Memorandum Submitted to the Canadian Royal Commission on Banking and Finance', Princeton University, *Essays in International Finance*, (May), pp.241-74.

Saul, S. B. (1969): *The Myth of the Great Depression, 1873-1896*, London: Macmillan.

Sbordone, Argia, and Kenneth Kuttner (1994): 'Does Inflation Reduce Productivity?', Federal Reserve Bank of Chicago, *Economic Perspectives*, (November/December), pp.2-14.

Selgin, George (1988): *The Theory of Free Banking: Money Supply under Competitive Note Issue*, Totowa, New Jersey: Rowman and Littlefield.

_____ (1994): 'Free Banking and Monetary Control', *Economic Journal*, Vol. 104 (November), pp.1449-59.

_____ (1995a): 'The Case for a 'Productivity Norm': Comment on Dowd', *Journal of Macroeconomics*, Vol. 17 (Fall), pp.733-40.

_____ (1995b): 'The "Productivity Norm" versus Zero Inflation in the History of Economic Thought', *History of Political Economy*, Vol. 27 (Winter), 705-35.

_____ (1996a): *Bank Deregulation and Monetary Order*, London: Routledge.

_____ (1996b): 'Hayek vs. Keynes on How the Price Level Ought to Behave', Unpublished.

Selgin, George, and Lawrence H. White (1994): 'How Would the Invisible Hand Handle Money?', *Journal of Economic Literature*, Vol. 32 (December), pp.1718-49.

Shields, Roger Elwood (1969): 'Economic Growth with Price Deflation, 1873-1896.' Dissertation, University of Virginia.

Smyth, David J. (1995): 'Inflation and Total Factor Productivity in Germany', *Weltwirtschaftliches Archive*, No. 131, pp.403-5.

Stamp. Josiah (1931): *Papers on Gold and the Price Level*, London: P. S. King & Son.

Tatom, John A. (1979): 'The Productivity Problem', Federal Reserve Bank of St. Louis *Review*, No. 61 (September), pp.3-16.

Taylor, John B. (1985): 'What Would Nominal GNP Targeting Do to the Business Cycle?', *Carnegie-Rochester Conference Series on Public Policy*, No. 22, pp.61-84.

Tsiang, S. C. (1969): 'A Critical Note on the Optimum Supply of Money', *Journal of Money, Credit, and Banking*, Vol. 1 (May), pp.266-80.

Uhr, Carl (1975): *Economic Doctrines of David Davidson*, Stockholm: Almqvist & Wiksell.

Viner, Jacob (1937): *Studies in the Theory of International Trade*, New York: Harper & Brothers.

Warburton, Clark (1951): 'The Misplaced Emphasis in Contemporary Business-Fluctuation Theory', in American Economic Association *Readings in Monetary Theory*, pp. 284-318, Homewood, Ill.: Richard D. Irwin.

Warren, George F., and Frank A. Pearson (1933): *Prices*, New York: John Wiley & Sons.

White, Lawrence H. (1987): 'Accounting for Non-interest Bearing Currency: A Critique of the Legal Restrictions Theory', *Journal of Money, Credit, and Banking*, Vol. 19 (November), pp.448-56.

_____. (1989): *Competition and Currency*, New York: New York University Press.

Yeager, Leland B. (1986): 'The Significance of Monetary Disequilibrium', *Cato Journal*, Vol. 6 (Fall), pp.369-99.

_____. (1992): 'Austrian Themes in a Reconstructed Macroeconomics', Unpublished typescript.

_____. (1996a): 'Injection Effects and Monetary Intermediation', in George Selgin, (ed.), *The Fluttering Veil: Essays on Monetary Disequilibrium by Leland Yeager*, Indianapolis: Liberty Fund (forthcoming).

_____. (1996b): 'New Keynesians and Old Monetarists', in George Selgin, (ed.), *The Fluttering Veil: Essays on Monetary Disequilibrium by Leland Yeager*, Indianapolis: Liberty Fund (forthcoming).

New Zealand's Remarkable Reforms

Donald T Brash

1. New Zealand's economy has revived in the last few years, following '…one of the most remarkable economic liberalisations in modern times' since 1984. There is little public enthusiasm for reversing the reforms.

2. Once one of the most regulated OECD economies, New Zealand is now one of the least regulated. Unemployment has recently fallen sharply. The estimated sustainable annual growth rate of real GDP is now 3-3½ per cent.

3. The transformation of New Zealand – from a protectionist, regulated society with 'cradle-to-grave' welfare to an open, market-based economy operating under the rule of law – has a 'Hayekian flavour'.

4. Under the guidance of Roger (now Sir Roger) Douglas, New Zealand adopted a 'big bang' approach to reform, though the pace of reform slackened for a time in the late 1980s.

5. Micro-economic reforms included removal of controls on wages, prices, and foreign exchange and floating of the New Zealand dollar. Import quotas have been removed and tariffs reduced. Agricultural and industrial subsidies have virtually disappeared.

6. '…the most remarkable liberalisation' has been that of the labour market where from 1991 contracts have been on '…almost the same basis as other commercial contracts'. By December 1995 only 17 per cent of the workforce had union-negotiated collective contracts.

7. High marginal rates of income tax have been reduced and a broad-based Value Added Tax introduced. The tax structure is now '<None>the least distorting of any in an OECD country'.

8. State-owned companies have been 'corporatised' and many have been privatised. Privatisation has generally not taken place until a corporation entered a contestable market: privatised companies are lightly regulated under the general powers of the Commerce Act.

9. A Fiscal Responsibility Act promotes sound fiscal policies and requires governments to explain present and projected budgetary positions.

10. Under the Reserve Bank of New Zealand Act of 1989, the government specifies an inflation target and the Bank Governor is left to implement it. The Governor can be dismissed for 'inadequate performance'. So far the monetary framework has been very successful in reducing inflation and inflationary expectations.

The Institute of Economic Affairs

2 Lord North Street, Westminster, London SW1P 3LB
Telephone: 0171 799 3745 Facsimile: 0171 799 2137
E-mail: iea@iea.org.uk Internet: http://www.iea.org.uk   ISBN 0-255 36400-8

£5.00

Back From the Brink: An Appeal to Fellow Europeans Over Monetary Union

Pedro Schwartz

1. European Monetary Union is an 'unprecedented experiment', a 'huge gamble' which produces mixed reactions among Europeans.

2. There are many possible pitfalls before monetary union can come into being. One particular problem is that from 1998 to 2001, national currencies will remain legal tender. The currencies of 'misbehaving countries' may therefore be '…pounced upon by speculators and marauders…'

3. A monetary zone can function effectively only if it encompasses a single market, especially a single labour market. Establishing a monetary union when there is no hope of removing some of the barriers to a single market means '…applying perpetual fetters'.

4. The labour market of the European Union is '…far from being integrated'. The entry into monetary union of countries with rigid labour markets would warp the functioning of the union: moreover, those countries would probably demand subsidies to alleviate unemployment.

5. European Monetary Union therefore faces 'a bumpy road' before and after 2002. Before 2002 there may be 'speculative storms'; after 2002 large pockets of unemployment may persist, undermining European unity.

6. If European politicians had really wanted a stable currency they would have linked their currencies to the Deutschmark and turned their Central Banks into currency boards.

7. Monetary competition among existing European currencies plus the euro would offer a better long run prospect of monetary stability than monetary union.

8. Competitive devaluation is less of a problem than industrial lobbies claim. Over-valuation is more of a danger: '…fake converts from easy virtue love the prestige of a strong currency'.

9. In practice, careful economic analysis of European Monetary Union 'counts for nothing'. The proposed union is a 'dangerous experiment…' to build a certain kind of Europe surreptitiously' and to give a '…huge boost to centralisation'.

10. If monetary union goes ahead, Britain should go it alone and '…set an example from within the European Union of what can be achieved by a competitive, deregulated, private economy with a floating and well-managed currency'.

The Institute of Economic Affairs

2 Lord North Street, Westminster, London SW1P 3LB
Telephone: 0171 799 3745 Facsimile: 0171 799 2137
E-mail: iea@iea.org.uk Internet: http://www.iea.org.uk   ISBN 0-255 36401-6

£4.00